TRIUNE GODDESS SHAKTHI

The untold story of Jesus and Mary Magdalene

Mario Perera
Laetitia Buczaczer

First published in 2017 by

Becomeshakespeare.com
Wordit Content Design & Editing Services Pvt Ltd
Unit - 26, Building A-1, Nr Wadala RTO, Wadala (East),
Mumbai 400037, India
T:+91 8080226699

Copyright © 2017 by Mario Perera & Laetitia Buczaczer
No part of this publication may be reproduced, stored in or introduced into a retrieval system, or transmitted, in any form, or by any means (electronic, mechanical, photocopying, recording or otherwise), without the prior permission of the publisher. Any person who commits an unauthorized act in relation to this publication can be liable for criminal prosecution and civil claims for damages.
Please do not participate in or encourage piracy of copyrighted materials in violation of the author's rights. Purchase only authorized editions.

©
ISBN: 978-93-86487-40-7

This book is dedicated to:

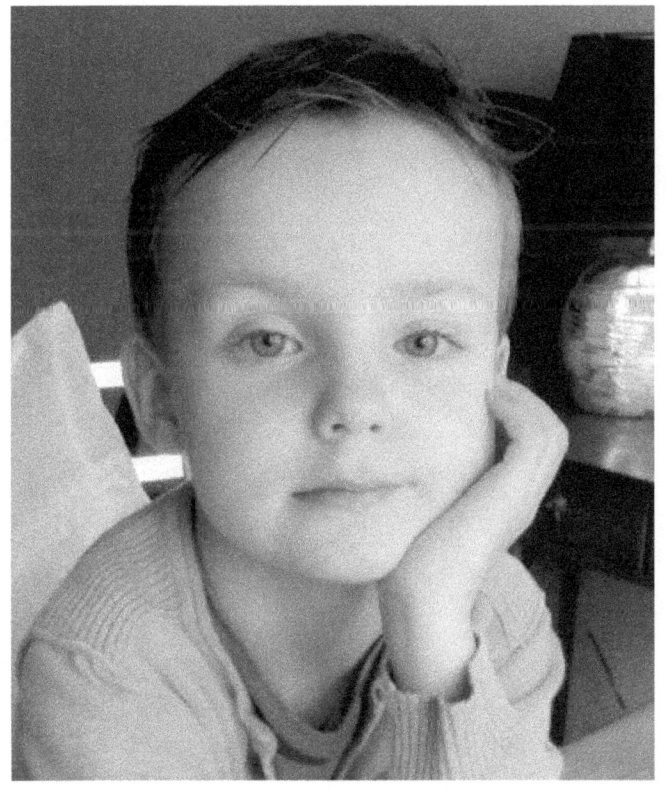

MAXENCE NEELKANTH

INTRODUCTION

Many are the works of fiction, some by world famous writers such as D. H. Lawrence, on the subject of Jesus. Yet this book is one with a difference. It seeks to unravel the enigma that was Jesus of Nazareth by a probe into his subconscious mind, the latent ever simmering mirror of the innermost self from which the external visible entity derives its form and existence on the passing scene of time.

While being essentially imaginative, the book incorporates a vast process of thought which includes philosophy, theology, biblical knowledge, insights from world religions, as well as ancient and recent history, in its narrative. Its motive is not to reinforce the belief of a particular religion's denomination, but to present a unique world religious figure in a manner that transcends religious, racial, cultural and historical horizons.

The Jesus of this book is not the historical person the Catholic and the Christian Churches propose to believers, but one who grapples with his identity and mission from within a fertile mind field related more to mythology than to history. Such a phenomenon is not limited by space and time. What transpires within it is uninterrupted and ongoing. For not a moment is the subconscious mind inactive. It is permanently plugged to the memory and imagination, and its domain is the realm of dreams.

This subconscious mind of Jesus, the book proposes, is one that derives its vitality from different sources: Jewish, Egyptian, Greek and Indian. From within these fields, as remembrances of an ancient past and visions of a distant future, the hidden testament of Jesus emerges and evolves, unhindered by physical and mental barriers.

However, the predominant quintessential element that permeates the subconscious mind of Jesus gives meaning to his existence and mission, is the sacred feminine. Without it, points out the book, Jesus is a void and empty apparition, a form without a soul. This work therefore unambiguously asserts that woman is the primordial being of the manifest world, the surrogate form of the Earth, the primeval life giving force that pervades both womb and tomb, out of which everything, including the personification of the divine issues, and into which everything returns to reemerge anew.

The divine feminine thereby emerges as the indispensable key in determining the real identity, mission and destiny of the man Jesus of Nazareth. This is a truly unique work. It challenges the reader to surmount indoctrination and fear in the search for the truth, a truth which essentially, unequivocally and unquestionably is individual and personal.

Dr. Juanita REETZ, Ph.D., University of Rochester,
New York, U.S.A
University of Heidelberg

TABLE OF CONTENTS

Chapter 1 –	History and Myth	11
	Where myth differs frlom history	13
Chapter 2 –	Lost in the temple	16
Chapter 3 –	Confrontation with the High Priests	22
Chapter 4 –	I AM	25
Chapter 5 –	The safety plan	30
Chapter 6 –	Journey to Egypt	35
Chapter 7 –	The Garden of Eden	38
Chapter 8 –	The nature of the world	45
Chapter 9 –	The Nile	50
Chapter 10 –	The mirror of the Nile	54
Chapter 11 –	Clash of civilizations	58
Chapter 12 –	Fundamental questions that arose	61
Chapter 13 –	God and the world	65
Chapter 14 –	God and man	70
Chapter 15 –	Man and woman	74

Chapter 16 –	Satan deceived	79
Chapter 17 –	doubts that appear	83
Chapter 18 –	Human or divine	88
Chapter 19 –	Temptations intensify	96
Chapter 20 –	God's identity by Imperial Decree	102
Chapter 21 –	Lesson of the pyramids	108
Chapter 22 –	Yearning for immortality	112
Chapter 23 –	Satan and Salvation	116
Chapter 24 –	Context of the gods	121
	Mother and son	124
	The enigma that is woman	125
Chapter 25 –	New earth: new creation	128
Chapter 26 –	Vanquishing death	132
Chapter 27 –	The question of God	136
Chapter 28 –	Questions requiring answers	142
Chapter 29 –	The cosmic form	145
Chapter 30 –	The many 'selfs'	150
Chapter 31 –	An unexpected meeting	155
Chapter 32 –	What others thought of him	158

Chapter 33 – What he thought of himself	164
Chapter 34 – Desert and mirages	168
Chapter 35 – Where is God?	171
Chapter 36 – Vision of glory	175
Chapter 37 – Light that is life	179
Chapter 38 – The glory of God	184
Chapter 39 – Back to the land of birth	188
Chapter 40 – Garden of Gethsamanee	191
Chapter 41 – Beginning that never ends	198
Chapter 42 – Nature of woman	201
Chapter 43 – Miriam	206
Chapter 44 – Parting that never was	211
Chapter 45 – Final chapter	216

CHAPTER 1 - HISTORY AND MYTH

He was known as the son of a carpenter. Joseph his father had worked on several Roman building sites that hired cosmopolitan labour. He had thus, as a boy, come in contact with people of the great nations: Egyptians, Greeks, Romans as well as people from India and other places of the East. He had sat by the firesides in the evenings along with his father and heard them spend their time fraternally discoursing with one another, and relating their stories. He had listened enthralled as he heard them narrate their religious myths.

Are myths really different from history? one had queried.

History was punctuated by dates and places. History is an archive mainly of past events. Once those archives were lost, then their content was gone, and so would the events they narrated. They could never more be recreated or reenacted. They would be irretrievably lost forever. These archives were not only written records, but also memory data.

He had heard some one in their discussion group say: *When an old man dies, it is a library that is burnt and reduced to ashes.*

What history is, depends on who expounds it, another had said.

History differs according to the causes rival parties, be they individuals or nations, espouse. The history that contemporaries of an era share, is not the history drafted for the study of the next generation. Such history was edited in such a manner that villains were made up into heroes, and sinners into saints.

Now he dwelt on the history of his own people. It struck him that when history was given a divine coloring, then murder, pillage, the sackings of cities, mass destruction, every art of violence, including the most gruesome atrocities, were accepted with the fervent belief that it is God's will that was being done on earth as it is in heaven. The history recounted in the Torah was proof of this grave assertion.

Do myths recount truths?

Myths were about truths and the truths the myths dwelt on were eternal. They had no beginning and no end. Should myths be lost, they would be recreated, because myths were the answers to the eternal questions the human mind, individual and collective, asked itself. They were not conditioned by time and space. They were not only about what occurs here below, but were also the closest man came to the above and the beyond. They were the oases that revived the spirit of man in the the desert of life, and kept him determined to reach his destination. They were the tips of the mountains that touched the sky. They reached out from the present like hands stretched out towards the unknown. They were arms outstretched heavenwards and not towards the visible horizons, the domain of time.

His present society too was saturated with stories of the divine, proceeding from great neighbouring civilizations. They all seemed so similar. The story of God coming to earth, being born of a virgin, manifesting a heroic, counter-cultural love toward outcasts, performing unbelievable miracles, dying for the people who killed him, and then rising from the dead, had a familiar "echo" to it. Hearing such stories had an effect on him that was somewhat like recalling a long forgotten dream.

On some level, there was a part of him that seemed to intuitively "remember" something when he came into contact with the loving saviour portrayed in those beliefs. Something within him sensed that these stories put him in touch with a dream about the way things are supposed to be. It reconnected him with something he had lost along the way, something he had perhaps given up on, something he had forgotten and which he was desparately trying to revive.

Where myth differs from history

Throughout history and in every culture, people have in a wide variety of ways recalled this dream. They expressed this dream through myths and legends. He realized that "myth" and "legend" are for most people equivalent to "untruth." But there was in his mind a much more profound sense in which myths and legends can be very true. At their best, myths and legends expressed his innermost sense of reality, his deepest longings, the obstacles he faced in pursuing these longings, and his hope that somehow, someday, these longings will be satisfied. In other words, myths and legends expressed to him a persistent dream that is as old as life itself, the dream of immortality. It is this yearning for immortality that myths bring to the fore. Myths ask the question: *why must man have to die?* The answers they provide are manifold. They express the common yearnings of mankind. Though expressed by the most diverse cultures and civilizations they are, unlike history, astoundingly consistent with one another.

In his own religious tradition death came into the world as the wage for sin. To undo the yoke of death, the eternal and infinite God himself conceived an elaborate plan. First and foremost he begot a son as eternal and infinite as himself and sent him to earth infused with his own Spirit. God's will with regard to his Son was clear – he had to die as atonement for man's original sin. After the death, resurrection and ascension into heaven of his son, God determined that his presence in the world should continue through his own Spirit: the Spirit that vivifies and enlilghtens all that exists. The scriptures of his religion written by priestly scribes made it out that God's entire existence was infused and imbued with one exclusive purpose and concern. It was all and only about man created from the dust of the earth.

God's entire existence was depicted as being centered from all eternity on man, his sin, the divine atonement, and salvation in the afterlife. It was to this end that God engendered a Son and produced a Holy Spirit, all three existing as ONE GODHEAD. Such was the importance of man to God. Indeed the only dream of God, as eternal and infinite as himself was made to appear as the desire of donning human flesh and entering the realm of time and space. Indeed it was not good for God – even a Triune God – to be alone.

And so the emissary of God, none other than God the Son was born directly through divine intervention and of a virgin who had to be the purest of women in the entire history of womankind. He had to live a life totally pleasing to God by doing God's will. Indeed being God he had no other choice. His mission was well defined. He had to repel the devil, the enemy of God and of humanity. But most of all he had to die as all humans do, as atonement for their fault. As reward for accomplishing the will of God, God would resurrect him from the dead, and remove the stigma of mortality from all human beings. And so death would finally be vanquished and made the gateway to immortal life in paradise for all.

All that humanity has to do to reap the benefit of the life and death of the God-man, is to choose him as its way, as its truth, and as its life. Thus humanity will merge with him, be one with him, and be pleasing to God as he was, meriting for itself the gift of immortality and life eternal.

CHAPTER 2 - LOST IN THE TEMPLE

Her name was Miriam and she was twelve years old. Being an orphan she had been confided to the care of the wife of the trustee of the synagogue of Magdala, a port city near Jerusalem. Due to the prevailing restrictions placed on women she had learned the Torah at home from her adoptive mother. At the time of the Passover, the family travelled to Jerusalem. They spent the days in the temple and the nights sleeping on make shift bedding within the sacred precincts.

She did not relish these visits. It was the domain of men. The men gathered together, held discussions, and engaged in various liturgical activities together, leaving the women folk to fend for themselves. In the meantime the women waited on their men, cooked their food, mended their clothes, and listened to their exploits and the on goings within the hallowed edifice.

Often left to her own, she wandered about the temple premises with her friends. They were specially attracted by the business activities taking place within them. On one such occasion she had noticed a boy of her own age strolling around the temple alone. Something inexplicable drew her to him. The attachment she felt towards him seemed irresistible and defied reasoning. She recalled a dream of being led by the hand and shown a sleeping figure whose form seemed to merge with the features of this boy. Dreams, she knew, played a preponderant role in the religious history of her people.

Since the first day she saw him, that particular dream intruded even into her dormant mind. This made her observe him all the closer. She noticed that he was not like others of his age. While the others spent their time as all children do, playing together and enjoying their limited freedom, this particular boy seemed to enjoy his solitude. What aroused her sympathy in his regard was that he did not seem to be accompanied by parents or kith and kin. He was alone. She approached her foster parents and informed them of her discovery. She was adamant that they make enquiries about his situation.

And so the three wound their way through the teeming thousands in search of the solitary boy. They found him seated on the ground, his eyes closed, closely following the prayer that was being recited. It was a particular psalm. They approached him and sat beside him. But he seemed oblivious of their presence. He was intoning for himself a stanza of that psalm. They were now listening with great attention to what he was reciting. This is what they heard.

For you created my inmost being; you knit me together in my mother's womb My frame was not hidden from you when I was made in the secret place, when I was woven together in the depths of the earth. Your eyes saw my unformed body; all the days ordained for me were written in your book before one of them came to be.

They were taken by surprise. The boy was very young, surely about the age of their foster daughter. If he was reciting that stanza it was because he understood its content. He was even transfixed and sunk in deep contemplation, almost in a trance.

The temple premises were now resounding with the public recital of the events of the Exodus. He was listening to the episode of the burning bush with deep concentration, and when the answer of the Lord regarding his holy name was declared ceremoniously, he was heard to repeat the phrase: *I AM WHO AM*, while all others listened in awesome silence. When the event of the parting of the Red Sea was being narrated, the child was seen to stretch out his right hand at the invisible ocean. This gesture left the parents of the little girl perplexed. All in all the presence of this solitary child and his attitude mystified them.

The boy then got up and began to walk. They followed him silently intent on learning more about him. His steps were measured and meditative. He was aware of all that transpired around him yet he did not seem distracted. Finally they decided to engage him in conversation. They gently asked him who he was, and he politely replied: Jesus, Jesus of Nazareth.

How old are you? they enquired.

Twelve years, he said.

How come you are alone? they asked.

It will not be for long he said. *My parents will soon find out that they have left me behind, and return.*

This is God's house and you appear to like being here, they remarked

Not particularly, he replied. Furthermore, *God is not confined to a temple*

But this temple contains the covenant between God and his people, they observed guardedly.

It is a covenant made with a god of a people and not with the God of all peoples, the boy said.

The parents of the little girl were baffled. They were even fearful lest passers by heard the boy speak.

We believe that this temple will endure forever as will also the covenant between god and his chosen people.

A day will come when not a stone upon a stone will remain of this temple. As for the covenant a new one will take the place of the present.

What will that be? They asked

It will be a tree, the boy said, *a tree of Enlightenment*

We know of a tree of good and evil whose fruit brought death and suffering to the world.

Not so the fruit of the tree of Enlightenment. It will offer release from suffering and death, the boy replied.

Tell us more about this tree, they said

Before answering, the boy's eyes assumed a distant look. He even seemed troubled. Finally as if in a dream, he replied: *It will be the simplest of trees, a bare trunk and a bare horizontal branch. But it will yield the fruit that will give eternal and immortal life to all.*

On being invited by the girl's parents, the little boy followed them and settled down with them in the little enclosure that was their temporary abode. He ate the food they offered him, and answered their numerous questions. They conversed late into the night. The boy had the makings of a revolutionary and a rebel, a fact which troubled the two elders. As for the little girl a curious magnetic current continued to bind her to the boy. It seemed to her that her dream had come alive. *How could it be when we are both just twelve years old?* she wondered.

As sleep descended on her so did her dream, but this time with more clarity and more details. She dreamt of a luscious garden where she was walking hand in hand with a bearded old man identified as the gardener. The garden she was told belonged to her and to her life companion. It was to him that she was being taken. Her imagination had by now created for her the image of her consort. Then she glimpsed from afar the sleeping figure of a young man.

This is he, the gardener was telling her.

Now she was standing over him, and saw him open his eyes awakened by the awareness of her presence. As their eyes met, mutual recognition dawned. *I knew you even before my eyes alighted on you*, she said in ecstatic delight.

And you are my dream come true, he answered with the same joyous reaction. And now they were looking at each other imbued with the same happiness as on that first meeting.

Eons had nows gone by, yet that first meeting was as present to them now as it had then been. The eternal NOW could not be obliterated by the passing scenes of time. They even seemed to hear the heavenly vault resounding with the intonation: *as it was in the beginning, now and ever shall be, world without end.*

We are no more in that garden of delights, my love, she said indicating to him that she knew what was transpiring in his mind. *But I will offer you more delights than what that garden could ever have given you,* she told him tenderly. *But you have still to ask me my name.*

I know your name, he answered softly. *You were Eve. Now you are Miriam.*

The next morning they heard a message being passed from mouth to ear. It was announced that the high priest and his assistants would be present in the body of the temple among the people to impart to them their blessings at the end of the festive season. And so the people were being invited to throng the great hall where the meeting was to take place. They never in their wildest imagination expected to see and hear what was about to take place.

~~~ ~~~ ~~~

CHAPTER 3 - CONFRONTATION WITH THE HIGH PRIESTS

The meeting with the priests took place as scheduled. Jesus was seated with the family from Magdala. The High priest addressed the gathering and said. We are assembled here because we all believe in God as a person.

Then, as if out of nowhere a soft voice cleaved the ensuing silence. *No, not I* the voice said. *I do not believe in such a God.*

All turned their heads in very direction to locate the origin of that voice. It was in vain, because the source of the voice remained hidden.

Who was it who spoke? the high priest asked.

It was then the fragile figure of a small boy rose up and showed himself.

How old are you boy? the high priest asked with a cynical expression on his face.

Twelve, the boy answered unflinchingly

The answer sent ripples of laughter among the group of priests. The laughter was intended to put the boy into derision among the onlookers of the unfolding drama. They succeeded somewhat because some of the crowd took the bait and began to giggle at the boy.

Why do you say that God is not a person? The highest temple dignitary asked him.

How do we conceive a person? The boy asked. We conceive a person as a 'he' or as a 'she'. God is none of them. He is also not a 'it'. God as a person is a projection of our minds. He is man made. As such he would incorporate all human insufficiencies, deficiencies, failings, faults and even sins. In fact such a one is the God of the Torah

What the boy uttered was pure blasphemy. The high priest however in a show of self mastery put up his hand and called for calm. When the agitation ceased the priest asked the boy How do you conceive God?

The word God referred to what human beings consider to be the infinite, the eternal and the immortal. God is THAT. 'That' being all that the mind cannot conjure. The unknown 'THAT' remains a mystery hidden from the human mind and inaccessible to it. All the mind's endeavours to grasp the content of 'THAT' are deceptive, hypnotic and seemingly magical, yet in the ultimate analysis, as sterile and empty as all thoughts.

Obviously irritated and embarrassed, the priests asked in sheer exasperation: are you saying that the teaching of the Bible is false?

You have said it, said the child. God by his very nature is hidden and impervious to the human mind. Strive as man may, and whatever be the subterfuges attendant on such striving, man cannot reveal the nature of God to other men.

The Bible does not say that a man revealed the nature of God to other men. What the bible says is that God himself did so.

Now who says that God revealed himself to men but man himself? So we are where we began and nothing has changed. There is no visible, audible, tactile being called God capable of giving information about himself to man, the boy answered.

You mean God can never appear in a human form? The priest asked.

What is a human form? The boy asked his interlocutors. Taken unawares by the question what prevailed was a deafening silence. The human form, the boy continued, is a sense object, an appearance in a continuous process of mutation. Being such, it has no reality. It is not real.

Then the Patriarchs, Moses, the prophets and the Messiah are all deluded individuals.

I would say so, the boy answered straightforwardly.

The heated debate between the aged high priest and the little boy had an electrifying effect on the listeners. The priest with his ceremonial sacerdotal regalia and seated on his high throne was seeing his hitherto uncontested supreme authority challenged fearlessly and derisorily. The unexpressed thoughts of the audience dwelt on the eventual fate of the little boy. They very thought made them shudder with apprehension.

CHAPTER 4 - I AM

✼✼ ✼✼

Visibly trying to raise his head after this head-on onslaught against his faith the high priest continued with his interrogation of the boy. Can man connect with God? He asked

The question is not about connecting but about identification, the boy answered. The moment we discover within us the divine consciousness, the light which is the life of men, then we really know who we are, because 'THAT' each one of us IS.

And who is 'THAT'? The priest asked, pushing him to utter his own words of self condemnation.

The boy was not deterred. Different civilizations answered this question differently. But all were agreed on one thing, that it was pure unmanifest Consciousness. May I state further, it is the 'That' we refer to by the name 'God'. Did not the psalm say: be still and know that I am God? That I is I. That I is each one of us. That unshakable infinite, eternal and immortal I is God.

What about the God in heaven, the one beyond, the one over and above, the one across the great divide? the priest asked.

The day my identity merges and fuses with the identity of God, that day the hidden God, the inaccessible God will cease to be the mystery that he presently is, because 'That' I AM.

The Torah does not teach such nonsense. From where did you learn this blasphemy? The priest's angry cry resonated within the halls of the temple.

The Torah is the work of priestly scribes. They had a choice to make and their choice was intentionally misleading. There were two trees in the Garden of Paradise that demanded their attention: the Tree of Good and Evil, and the Tree of life. They made the Tree of Good and Evil eclipse the Tree of Life, the only one that counted.

The discourse of the boy had now taken a personal tone. It was assailing the integrity of the priestly function. He had jolted the assembly into total wakefulness. All eyes and ears were now turned towards him. All felt the great tension that pervaded the atmosphere.

Give me the Torah, the boy said, and someone tendered the book to him. He opened the pages and was now fixing his attention on the text. Then he read out selected verses.

The devil told Adam and Eve: for God knows that when you eat of this fruit your eyes will be opened, and you will be like God, knowing good and evil. And so they did eat of it. Then the Lord God said, See, the man has become like one of us, knowing good and evil; and now, he might reach out his hand and take also from the tree of life, and eat, and live forever.

Let us not close our eyes before the obvious, the boy said turning towards the assembly. *Man had only to reach out his hand and pluck from the tree of life and he would have become immortal. Eating the fruit of that tree would have meant being assimilated into the divine consciousness. It would have meant the awareness that man is God. It was this truth that the priestly scribes hid from mankind.*

Now man knows good and evil. He has ever since remained mesmerized by the tree of good and evil staring at the serpent offering him its fruit. His sole concern is good and evil. He spends his mortal life engaged in an eternal and everlasting unsuccessful struggle to conquer evil. His total attention and concentration being with the tree of good and evil he lives entirely within its horizons.

The presence of the other tree within him has faded into oblivion. Yet the fruit of that tree beckons to him from within the innermost depths of his mind and heart with the words: be still and know that I am God. *Embroiled as he is in good and evil, this truth, man cannot perceive and see. For as Isaiah said,* "he has blinded their eyes and he has hardened their heart, so that they would not see with their eyes and perceive with their heart".

You do not seem to like us, the high priest now said adopting a more conciliatory tone. *Could you tell us why?*

The boy's reply was immediate and without the least trace of ambiguity: *because the God you have installed in this temple is a God of your making, a God who places you in your seats of power, and decorates you with halos of glory. Thus have* you have transformed the house of my father into a den of thieves.

The priest was now seething with rage. Before pronouncing judgment on the boy he nevertheless had one last question: *Is there anyone else in this gathering who shares the views of the boy,* he asked looking menacingly at those before him. Now total silence prevailed, a silence in which the least pin drop would have made noise. It was then that a little arm shot up.

I agree with him, someone said. It was a girl of the same age as the boy.

You are a female. How dare you intervene? the priest reprimanded her severely. You are not a person, you have no voice, he barked.

Do we need to hear more? The high priest asked re-affirming his authority.

No, no, stooges from within the crowd cried back.

Are the parents of his boy among us at this moment? the high priest asked.

It was then that there was heard the rustling of clothes as a woman and a man discretely rose up from where they sat. All eyes were now on them as they made their way through the throng towards the dais on which the priests sat.

Take away this little dreamer from my sight, the high priest told them in an enraged tone. *It is his age that has saved him from my just wrath.*

Joseph and Miriam made inaudible apologies to the offended hierarchy. The mother then pressed the child against her body and they softly retraced their way through the crowd to the courtyard below. The little girl and her parents had done the same and so they met. The children served as the glue that now bound the parents together.

Let us leave this place soon, the father of the little girl advised the group.

Then they quickly intermingled with the crowd and vanished from the sight of all. On reaching the main path leading away from the temple they searched for a caravan heading for Nazareth. On arriving at Nazareth and on being invited to do so, the little girl and her parents stayed over in the home of Mary and Joseph for the night.

CHAPTER 5 - THE SAFETY PLAN

✖ ✖   ✖ ✖

The events that had transpired in the temple troubled the peace of mind and tranquility of the respective parents of the two children. Rumours of that event continued to persist. News had even reached them that the priests had directed spies to trace the whereabouts of the boy. His parents felt deeply anguished, not knowing what step to take. It was in such a state of mind that they fell asleep that night. But the sleep of Joseph was disturbed by what was apparently the vision of an angel.

I come to you with a message from the Most High, the angel told him.

Joseph, who had assumed a suppliant attitude listened attentively.

Then the angel repeated the words entrusted to him. The message was contained in one simple line: *to Egypt my son must go.*

It was to Egypt that they had gone at the first threat to the boy's life. It was to Egypt they would now go with his life in danger once again. So would the little girl. There was no time to be wasted.

That night Jesus had no sleep. He lay awake for hours before finally making his way to the little courtyard in front of his home. His mind went over and over again to the thought of God. The two events uppermost in his mind were the slaughter of the Egyptians' infants by God's angel of death, and the slaughter of the Jewish infants by the soldiers of Herod Antipas. The first infanticide, the scriptures said, had as their goal the liberation of the chosen people from their bondage in Egypt. The second had as its goal the elimination of the Messiah who was the threat to Herod's kingship. In the second case the angel's warning prevented the hand of death striking the infant Messiah, but other infants made the supreme sacrifice for his preservation. His parents had narrated to him the horrendous incident in every gruesome detail.

Having heard the story of the dreams his mother and his foster father had in his regard, he became aware that he was the apparent cause of so many infant children losing their lives. That sense of guilt weighed so heavily on his mind that he would wake up in the night on hearing a voice and in a state of intense anguish, his body soaked in sweat. *The voice in Ramah was of weeping and great mourning, Rachel weeping for her children and refusing to be comforted, because they are no more.*

But that is not all, a voice said. What about the first born of the Egyptians smitten by the angel of death the emissary of God, so that Moses could lead his people out of Egypt, and thus create the bloodline out of which you emerged? His torment was unbearable. What was most oppressive however was the thought that relentlessly kept impinging on his mind that he would have to expiate in his lifetime for all the deaths of which he was the unwitting cause. Yet his whole being rebelled against that thought. How could he accept a God involved in such events? How could he accept any mission imposed on him by such a God?

The most radical question yet that he was now facing was, how can such a ruthless tyrant be 'God'? What could he be? A duplicate gone wrong? A false copy? A caricature? The only answer he could muster was that such a God could only be one made according to the image and likeness of man. If the writers of such narratives could conceive of such a God, it would be an abominable violation of the very first divine commandment, the ground on which his people lived, moved and had their being. Yet the real problem lay elsewhere. They put in doubt the very source of the dreams his mother and foster father had experienced in his regard. He did all he could to escape these torments. Yet what better way could he find than by taking refuge in dreams?

It was then that he heard the muffled sound of feet coming out of the house. They were those of the girl. She approached him and sat by his side. He felt her hand on his and heard her say: *I know you are troubled. I also know the anguish you feel and why. We are in this together. I will not leave you alone. I will be accompanying you to Egypt tomorrow.*

He did not know how much she knew of his life. Yet he had an uncanny feeling that she was much more than a casual acquaintance. Her actions and reactions as well as her attitudes seemed to him to evoke memories of a long transpired past. He recalled the scene in the temple and the total solidarity she had manifested in his regard. She had stood by his side, against the incomparable odds that were pitted against him. Theirs was not a chance encounter.

Jesus was now telling Miriam what was foremost in his mind.

Miriam, do you still remember what the hight priest told my parents?

I do, she anwered. What he told you was more than something said in anger. It was a revelation.

A revelation? Jesus asked in a perplexed tone of voice.

Yes, Miriam replied calmly. He called you a dreamer. Jesus, the history of our people is the story of a dream.

On hearing the words of Miriam, the spaces of his mind opened and he saw his personal history unfold. He felt his form being metamorphosed into that of the patriarch Joseph. It was all happening to him. The dream was coming alive. It was now become a vision tearing asunder the veil that was the darkness of the night. He saw the sun, the moon, and eleven stars bowing to him, acknowledging his supremacy. His dream had led him, and through him his entire people, to Egypt. His form was continuing to metamorphose and merged with that of Moses. It was another dream like happening, the vision of a burning bush, that impelled him to lead his people out of Egypt, to a land of dreams called the promised land. It was dreams and visions that had given him his existence as Jesus. Dreams had led him once again to Egypt. It would also be dreams that would lead him out of Egypt to open the way to another dream, a promised land that would enflame and set alight the dream of mankind. Indeed all the saviours of humanity had coalesced into one being which was his person. Out of the one proceeded the many and the many retraced their steps to the one. Awareness had dawned on him that HE was that ONE.

Soon worn out by their restless minds, they fell asleep together in the open courtyard. In their sleep, their consciousness merged into one and they were engulfed in the same dream world, a world that was a luscious, blooming, and fruit filled garden. He saw himself asleep and felt like a woman in labour. He was feeling the intense pain of childbirth. What he then saw was his rib cage being rent open and a form, that of a woman emerge from within his heart. As she stood before him the pain turned into an intense joy and happiness. He was telling her: *you are flesh of my flesh and bone of my bone.* He stretched out his arms to hold her and take her into his embrace. When his mother moved by a premonition came in search of him not finding him in the house, she saw him asleep with his arms around the young woman. She tiptoed back to her place and spent the rest of the night seated and engrossed in intense thought.

~~~ ~~~ ~~~

CHAPTER 6 - JOURNEY TO EGYPT

The very next day Joseph went to Sepphoris, the city the Romans were building, and contacted a caravan that plied regularly between that city and Egypt. And so it came to pass that the two families embarked on one such caravan and headed for Egypt. After several days of travel they came to Egypt. There they alighted from the caravan and made their way on foot to the nearest city. Arriving at a cross-road they paused not knowing which way to proceed. As they stood perplexed, Miriam held Jesus by his hand and said: *this way.*

Why my child? Mary asked surprised by her initiative.

Someone who is awaiting our arrival, she replied.

And so they walked on until a temple loomed ahead. With calm determination Miriam led the group towards it. As the temple came into full view they saw a woman, a priestess, dressed in her liturgical robes standing on the threshold. Now they stood directly before her.

She has been waiting for us, the little girl said.

As if answering their unasked question, the priestess was saying: *I have been in communion with the Mother Goddess whose temple this is. Even at this moment I am possessed by her and I hear her telling me: behold my son.* And so she embraced him before the amazed eyes of his parents, and took him unto her own.

After days spent with their children in the home of the priestess, the time had now come for the parents to depart. The boy and the girl clung to each other refusing to be separated. The situation was heart rending.

Do not be anguished, the priestess told the parents. *This is what the spirit of God had willed, that they be together, just as they were in the beginning.*

Then, as if under a sudden stroke of inspiration she took the Torah from a desk. Turning to them she told them: *this is your sacred book. Now go to your God for guidance. Open it and read what your eyes alight on.*

They opened the Torah and read the verses that immediately propped up before their eyes, hoping to see the will of God in their regard. The verses their glance alighted on read as follows:

But Ruth said, *"Do not urge me to leave you or turn back from following you; for where you go, I will go, and where you lodge, I will lodge. Your people shall be my people, and your God, my God. Where you die, I will die, and there I will be buried. Thus may the LORD do to me, and worse, if anything but death parts you and me."* ...

The elders now looked at each other with looks of mystification. Then the priestess spoke. *These two children have old souls in new human forms. Their relationship goes back to an unimaginable past. This is obvious from the fact that they love one another 'even as the Lord loves'. So what God has joined together, let no one put asunder.*

The parting of parents and children brought unbearable grief to all, but all realized that the hand of God was upon the little boy and the little girl, and that through them his will would be done on earth as it is in heaven.

The return journey to Nazareth of Mary and Joseph was enveloped in silence. Their minds were besieged by thoughts. Their nights were sleepless. No words were exchanged between them, yet one knew what the other was engrossed with. On the final night of the journey Joseph whispered words of consolation and hope to his wife.

Mary, he said, *our son will grow in age as other children do, but you will not be with him to teach him wisdom.*

Yes I will .Joseph, she said. *My role will be assumed by another. That other will have my nature and bear my name. Our son will drink from that fountain of wisdom.*

Their unspoken thoughts were uttered through an unspoken word: Miriam. Now what the mother felt was a transformation. Her form and that of her man were undergoing a metamorphosis. The Miriam who had assumed her place and was speaking to the man by her side was telling him: *Jesus, where you go, I will go, and where you lodge, I will lodge. Your people shall be my people, and your God, my God. Where you die, I will die, and there I will be buried. Thus may the LORD do to me, and worse, if anything but death parts you and me.*

CHAPTER 7 - THE GARDEN OF EDEN

Years had passed since they had first arrived in Egypt. The land of Egypt was not strange to them, Moreover on more than one count Egypt was also their land. It was here the youngest son of the patriarch Jacob was brought as a slave. He later assumed the most exalted position as a deputy of the Pharaoh himself. It was also here that the entire community of Jews was eventually reduced to slavery and finally rescued by Moses under the leadership of God himself. Jesus knew the Torah well. However the books that most absorbed his attention were those of Genesis and Exodus.

One night as they sat together in the courtyard of their foster mother, Jesus suddently turned towards Miriam and asked: *Miriam, do you still remember our dream life in the garden of Eden*? Now he was listening enraptured as the story unfolded. What he heard was the voice of Miriam but the form he saw was that of another.

Well, Eve was telling her children, I will tell you the story of a dream that I had. I dreamed that I was the only woman on earth and that I was living in a big and very beautiful garden. It was a wonderful orchard with every kind of luscious fruit almost ready to fall into my mouth and into that of your father. Now how can there be a garden without a gardener? I asked myself. So I imagined a gardener who was able to describe the garden to us.

I asked your father, what name shall we give him? So we imagined a nice name for him. We called him God. Your father and I were the only human beings in that garden and the gardener would have authority over us. He would have the power to keep us within the garden or send us out of it. Our well being and protection depended on him. We put all our sentiments of dependence and protection in his regard in that name.

Did he like that name mother? the children asked.

Well, he did not seem to object, but I notice a frown that appeared on his forehead. Coming from you I will accept it, he said, but I foresee problems arising in due time.

What sort of problems? I ventured to ask.

Well, this entire story is your edition, is it not? He said. He continued further. Like all stories this too will be subject to revision. You consider it to be a dream. Other editors will call it real. Still others will call it history, myth, legend and so on and so on. With each new edition and revision the actors too undergo changes and subject themselves to the most varied interpretations and viewpoints. So the name you give me could well become a subject of conflict between men.

But let us get on with our story. Any questions? he enquired.

Can we eat all the fruit of this garden? I asked him.

The gardener told us that we could eat of the fruit of all the trees save one. It was the tree of the knowledge of good and evil. The point is that we knew only the good. So it was natural that we wanted to know whatever else there was to know. That was what our reason told us. However, I asked the gardener:

Why are you forbidding us to eat the fruit of that tree? It was then that he introduced new ideas into our relationship with him, which had escaped my mind.

Well, he said you call me God which means you accept that I made you. It is therefore reasonable to think that I know better what is good for you. That stands to reason. Does it not?

Yes, I replied. Indeed, that stands to reason. If as you say you made us then you would certainly know what is good for us.

What happened then, mother? the children asked, keen to know the continuation of the narrative.

Well, my curiosity continued to trouble me. It even grew in leaps and bounds. We had just come to know that there was something called evil, though we did not know what it was. In the same way could there be anyone else besides him and us in this garden? Was there someone God did not want us to know? The intrigue was all the greater having been made aware that he did not want us to know evil.

That question played incessantly on my imagination. It conjured up forms of that other whom God did not want us to know. Those forms became so vivid and powerful in my mind that they became irresistible. Why had God endowed our minds with imagination if it was bad to entertain the forms of its making? Now could such forms come to life? And so my imagination got the better of my reason and conjured up a form, a subtle form, a creepy one, one that would make the undergrowth his domain hoping that God himself would not see it. That form quietly evolved into that of a long round figure without arms and legs and came to life before my very eyes. So the form of my imagination had come to life.

Who are you? I asked him.

Call me serpent, he said. He then paused for a moment and said, well now that you called the gardener God if you wish you may call me 'devil'.

That opened my eyes. God is not the only one who can create, I thought, that I too can do, with my imagination. Having created the form of the serpent, the devil, the rest followed seamlessly. One last question to you, I told the bizarre figure. Where do you really live. God said he lives in heaven, and you?

Well, shall we say hell? In any case, does it matter? He answered. Both heaven and hell and their overlords, call them God or devil, are inconceivable to your minds.

I strained my mind to understand that, but it only gave me a violent headache. But we are here in paradise, a duplicate heaven. So how can you be here because your place is hell?

Well, the devil said after a reflective pause. It is really not the layout that matters but what happens within it that makes it heaven or hell.

One day as your father and I were passing by that tree, the one with the forbidden fruit, that creature of my imagination showed up before us. He was gliding up the tree and had plucked a fruit. This fruit he tendered to me.

No, I said, I cannot. God told us not to eat of it. Should we eat of it, he told us that we will die.

Now do not be stupid, the serpent told us. You know there are always two sides to a story. Now you only know one side of your story, and that is God's side. Once you eat this fruit you will also know the other side which is my side. That is fair. Do not forget that God is just and fair. Anyone who is good must also be just and fair. You have the right to know the complete story. That stands to reason, he wound up.

Strengthened by his wise words I bit into the fruit and ate a morsel. It was delicious. I then gave it to my husband who through love for me ate from it himself. Just then I heard the voice of God. Previously I heard the voice proceeding from the physical form of the gardener. But now he was only a voice.

You will never again see my form, he said. From now on no one can see my form and live. So I will only be a voice to you unless and until I decide otherwise. There is another matter you must know. You saw me until now. You heard me. You felt me when I took your hand in mine. I appealed to your reason and not to faith. What you see, hear and touch is what feeds your reason. But your reason could not restrain you. Your imagination proved to be the greatest force and the guiding light of your life. You wanted to know the other side of the story. It was your imagination that led the search. Henceforth let it be so. Let your imagination show you the way back to this garden and to me.

Well, I said to him, it was my imagination that conjured up everything within my mind. Could it be possible that my imagination reproduce every single feature and detail of my actual dream?

I doubt it, God said.

What happened then mother, the son asked.

Well then I woke up. The garden was gone and so was God. The serpent too had disappeared. And now I cannot even remember the dream, the mother confessed. Furthermore, I find so many gaps in that story and I must use my imagination to fill them up. In fact the dream has been replaced entirely by other forms and figures, by other words, ideas and actions of my imagination. So what my dream God said was right, I mean about editions and versions, interpretations and viewpoints. They are so varied and multifarious that a time might come when we would be forced to adopt one version by imperial or state law and under threats of severe punishments, even death. However, I tend to think that the greatest dissuasive force will be the threat of eternal damnation in hell.

Well, if devils dole out luscious apples, hell would not be too bad a place either, my children said.

As the familiar scene vanished from his mind, he felt that he was groping in the dark. What resonated in his mind were the words proffered by Eve: *But we are here in paradise, a duplicate heaven. So how can you be here because your place is hell? Well,* the devil said after a reflective pause. *It is really not the layout that matters but what happens within it that makes it heaven or hell*

~~~ ~~~ ~~~

CHAPTER 8 - THE NATURE OF THE WORLD

✼✼ ✼✼

That scene had changed and with it the stage set-up. What they confronted now was the final act of that same drama. Judgment had fallen on the human race. They now lived in a different dispensation on the passing scene of time and space. On that scene everything was destined to rise and fall, to appear and disappear, to live and to die. That lot was their's as well. There was no escaping it. It was still a woman's voice that resounded on the stage of his life: wherever you are, wherever you be, and whosoever you be, I will search for you and I will find you.

These were the last words he would hear as he lay on his deathbed. Paradise was a dream they had lived together. Now they were on earth as dust in human form infused with life. '*Dust you are and unto dust you will return*' was their human destiny engraved in the core essence of their very existence. So you will wander from life to life until the saviour appears in your very form. You will be wanderers on the face of the earth and never be still. Just as your bodies, so also your minds and hearts will undergo the throes of change, continuous and incessant, like the particles of dust that you are, wafted by the winds.

Dust is the most ubiquitous element in nature. It is never still, always moving and never confined to a particular space. Its spaces are endless. Its wafting is never a measure of time, being invisible. One feels it, but never knows from where it comes, where it goes and what it becomes. Composed of dust, formed of dust, and disintegrating into dust, such is also the destiny of the human body. Restless like dust, restlessness is its name. As the body, so also its mind, a perfect reflection of the body's condition, never still, always restless and roaming with no definite and stable space or time references, with never a place of rest. He foresaw a day when he would say: *the son of man has no pillow to lay his head on.*

What holds us to a particular form amidst these incessant changes are memory and imagination. The memory and the imagination are therefore the buoys that hold that totality together. All mythologies speak of two rivers, that of oblivion and of knowledge. The one wipes out the slate of memory while the other restores it fully.

As for Jesus his memory did not seem limited to the form resulting from his birth. Dreams and visions continued to assail his awakening memories and remembrances making them present before his mind as actual realities. He came to the realization that he was the pivotal actor, the corner stone of the narratives of the scriptures. His mind did not conceive them as being past events. They were present in a fixed immovable now. He came to the consciousness that neither time nor space had any hold on him. But seeing himself, agonizing in the throes of death he was restless and apprehensive.

When the one Eve and the one Adam entered the world of multiplicity and splintering, their paths separated or seemed to be so. The one way became the many ways. There were no more one way, one truth and one life, but the many ways, the many truths and the many lives. The one seemed illusory and the many seemed to be the real. This was all in the changing reflections in the mirror of time and space. Nothing was anymore one, but many.

Eve, he cried out in sheer desperation, Eve, where are you?

I was Eve in the dream world that was the Garden of Eden my love, a woman's voice replied soothingly. Here, on this earth, the earth in its temporal condition, I am Miriam.

We never left the dream world Eve, Jesus said. You are Eve transformed. You are Eve become Miriam. You have undergone several transformations Eve, he continued. You personify the Earth the primordial life giving force. Initially formless and void, the creative power within you revealed itself as a woman's womb. Out of that earthen womb man came into being. It was out of your womb that I was born.

Eve, the man was telling her, you the eternal lover are also my mother and companion. But you are also flesh of my flesh and bone of my bone. The dictate of flesh and blood is that we unite and be one. So are we lovers. Finally, it is to you in your primordial form as earth that I will return and out of which I will rise again. So you are my womb and my tomb. From womb to tomb we will never leave each other but cleave to each other as one.

My journey from womb to tomb will not end with one life. We will seek each other during all our existences. The tomb will never be a final resting place because it will never exhaust its primordial function as the womb of the primordial man that I am. And then in my deep sleep I will call out to you in my dream, and out of my dream you will rise as lover, mother and companion.

He knew that Miriam had been following everything that was transpiring within him. When she finally spoke it was a confirmation that he had not been alone in the spaces of his mind.

You are right, Miriam said. We are both a dream, Adam. We and our world are a dream for what passes is nothing else but a dream. So too with the transient entity that is the dreamer. He too passes and therefore is himself a dream. But that is not all. If the dreamer is himself a dream, then whose dream is he? Is the Unmanifest Dreamer a force, a power, a person? Or yet still is it an Awakened One who is himself the stage and the actors of his own dream?

Miriam, the man was answering. I remember lying asleep on what seemed to be a giant serpent whose coils were heaving like the waves of the eternal waters. And so was I dreaming a dream. And in my dream I felt a form surging out of my navel and fastened to an umbilical cord. The form was calling out to me by name. On hearing that voice and on opening my eyes I saw that the form was the earth. The form that the earth had assumed was your form, Eve:

that form was you. It is you who usher in the light of day after the darkness of the night. It is you who rise as the morning dawning, fair as the moon, bright as the sun. It is you who bring God's dream to life.

Adam, she said, we are the actors on the stage of dreams. Only the conscious power of which each of us is a manifestation is real and true, nothing else. All that we now are, are elaborate results of the power of our imagination. Our world is the world of our imagination. It is our imagination that makes us glimpse the truth and the real, whatever be the name by which we call it.

CHAPTER 9 - THE NILE

So Jesus was back again in Egypt. The very word exercised a fascination with him, He associated Egypt with four principal features: the desert, the pyramids, the Red Sea, and the Nile. Egypt was a gift of the Nile. But Egypt was also the permanent mirage of the desert. It was in the desert that water flowed out of rocks on being struck by a magic wand, and bread sweetened with honey rained down from the sky. It was the mirages of the desert that begot the gods of Egypt. The mirages being many so were the gods. The religion of Egypt was therefore called polytheism. Now dreams and visions made him relate the desert with the Torah, for out of the Egyptian desert came forth the greatest book of the Torah, the Exodus.

Indeed Judaism was a branch that had torn itself away from the mighty perennial trunk that was polytheistic Egypt. Henceforth the breakaway branch did everything in its power to distinguish and differentiate itself from its mother tree, Egypt. Its principal ground of identity was what it recognized as being monotheism. Monotheism was the foundation, the columns and the roof of Judaism. The first and foremost of the Mosaic laws could therefore be none other than: *I am the Lord thy God, thou shall not have other gods but ME.*

Yet, the influence of the motherland could not be eliminated by laws, even those considered to be divine. The God of the Torah was never the one and only God the Torah presented him as being. He was a God who was a living contradiction. He was a God in search of his identity. He was a God who said he loved human beings even more than a mother-to-be loved the foetus in her womb. Yet that very same God did not have the slightest scruples about having to kill the first born of mankind. He was a God of love and of hate, a God of anger and vengeance. He was a God who created and destroyed. He represented the great diversity of qualities embodied in the Egyptian pantheon. The God of the Torah was the personification of the many. Indeed to avoid the least semblance of confusion, God prohibited the setting up of statues and images bearing his name. Behind this law was the fear that he would be seen for what he really was, the many. This was a fundamental lesson that the Egyptian desert taught Jesus.

Apart from the desert, Egypt had no existence without the Nile. Every year waters gush down, making the river swell and overflow. Then, as soon as the waters subside, the hot sun upon the mud deposited on the river banks brings fertility to the soil, and with it everything that a people can desire. Indeed, the water of the river is so delicious, that it is said that those who have once tasted it are always longing to drink it again. The Nile provided the waters of life to the Egyptian people. Egyptians watched the river filling up and emptying itself year after year as a sign of immortality.

Everything about Egypt was intimately and essentially linked with the yearning and desire for immortality. This was the truth the spirit within him weaved into his human form, that the waters of his body born of mother earth and impregnated with divine consciousness, were the waters of eternal life. With this thought a new scene had emerged. He heard himself telling a woman standing before him as he sat on the wall enclosing a well: *the waters I give you will never make you thirst again.*

And now he was seeing the Nile as having been his cradle and protector. He had on a previous stage scene been placed on the waters of the river among its bulrushes in a wicker basket to escape the edict of the ruler, that every newborn male Israelite be eliminated. The one who watched over him as he lay helpless on the waters was a woman. Her name was Miriam. She had seen to it that no harm befell him, and so saved him from his predicament, preserving him for the great event that was the Exodus from Egypt. He also remembered how the waters of the Nile transformed itself into blood in compliance with his command, to bend the Pharaoh's will, and how the Red Sea that received the waters of the Nile parted at his command, to let him and his people through. Indeed his life was linked with the waters.

It was then he felt his imagination wafting him forward in time. The spaces within him were now reverberating with the words: You saw the waters turned into blood. The day will come when you will turn water first into wine before transforming it into blood. Water to wine, wine to blood: the blood of eternal life.

Whose blood would that be? he was asking.

Yours, said the sound coming from afar. Your blood the life giving waters will become drinkable like wine.

What effect will that wine have on those who drink of it?

The same effect that the river Mnemosyne had on those who drank of it. It will restore their memory to its pristine state and they will remember.

What would that remembrance be?

That remembrance, each who drink of your chalice will express in one single phrase: THAT: I AM.

You are the divine source. Call it Mnemosyne, call it Nile, it is the identity that matters and not the name by which we call it. Your chalice will reveal to them their true identity and nature. As the *Orphic Hymn to Mnemosyne* said. *They will remember what they once knew.*

Now it was his own voice that he heard: *Whoever drinks from my chalice shall become as I am and I myself will become he, and the hidden things will be revealed to him.* The Last Supper of wine and bread will thus become an act of remembrance: He heard him addressing the apostles with the words: "*Do this in remembrance of me.*"

CHAPTER 10 - THE MIRROR OF THE NILE

While he continued glancing into the waters, he saw a vision emerging out of it which he was sensing as being an experience of real life. He saw a man he identified as Nicodemus coming to him at night. He was asking to be shown the path to immortality. Jesus heard his own voice as it said: *I tell you the solemn truth, unless a person is born of water and the spirit, he cannot enter the kingdom of God – the realm of immortality.*

Nicodemus said to him, *How can a man be born when he is old? He cannot enter his mother's womb and be born a second time, can he?*

Yes, Jesus told him, *you must enter your mother's womb and be born a second time.*

But he made a precision. The womb concerned was not the womb of his immediate biological mother, but the prototype of all maternal wombs: the life giving waters. Now Jesus showed him the beginnings, and Nicodemus saw the waters and the spirit hovering over them, and he heard the spirit say: *let there be light, the light that was the light of men.* Jesus showed him the nexus between the spirit, the waters of life, and LIGHT.

Nothing can be clearer on the subject than the very first verses of the Book of Genesis: *the Spirit of God moved over the waters and God said let there be LIGHT.* Thus the waters became LIGHT and light is the LIFE of men. The spirit was the divine consciousness while the waters were the mirror that reflected the image and likeness of the spirit. They were the feminine face of God for it was out of the feminine that arose life that is the light of men.

The waters were really the moving spheres of time and space or simply the earth and the heavens, in which the spirit would take its abode and become manifest. So he said: *I tell you the solemn truth, unless a person is born of water and spirit, he cannot enter the kingdom of God.* The waters by their very nature removed all traces of their past life and prepared the traveler for his future life, unburdened with attachments to earth.

Nicodemus was now seated at his feet and listening to his teaching. Your real identity lies in that light of the spirit, the light that is the divine consciousness and which is the real and true life of men. To reach immortality you must reach enlightenment which you will achieve and attain by retracing your path through the waters which is the mirror of time, into the divine consciousness and its stillness. Beyond that mirror lies the mystery that is the Godhead. *Now you see as if in a mirror. Then you will see face to face, the same face with the same eyes.* What you will undergo is a transfiguration, a rebirth into the divine nature.

The waters that Jesus was indicating were indeed living waters, for out of them surged the forms of Rebecca and

Rachel. Their meetings with their future husbands had a profound impact on the history of the chosen people. That history he realized, pointed directly to him. He had been present when they made their appearances each at a well. It was there that his surrogate forms of Isaac and Jacob met them and wooed them. As for Rachel he saw himself rolling the stone away, then kissing her and weeping aloud. Such was the joy and happiness of his vision of those feminine forms that had woven the strands of what would constitute the physical features and the identity of Miriam.

Now his attention turned to the melting snows upon the mountains far south, which were the sources of water for the Nile. This recollection exploded within his inner spaces like the winds of a mighty hurricane, that wafted him to snow clad Himalayan mountain peaks. Those were peaks of extraordinary heights, from where a different people of a different culture, race, and religion acclaimed him as the God of life and death. The stone hard icy cold snow capped peaks were hard and cold as death, but the melting snow now become water was the source of life.

That water transformed into a holy river flowed through their entire land like an umblical cord bringing life, prosperity, and well being to all. Considered as being the passage to immortality, it was through that holy river that the souls of their dead would make their way from darkness to the everlasting light of divine consciousness. The river, the symbol of the moving spheres of the earth and the heavens, was the womb out of which that new life would emerge.

In Jesus form and spirit were one. In him the spirit, moving over the waters was creating the form that served his needs and purposes at the relevant times and in the relevant spaces. The body of Jesus was not one once and for all. But he was for all: all nations and peoples, in all places and at all times. The physical form of Jesus was at the continual disposal of the spirit. That spirit is reality and truth. Everything else is illusion. The reality outside, the one generated by the union of time and space was illusion. Jesus, his physical form being in the hands of the spirit, was not contained within the limitations of space and time.

CHAPTER 11 - CLASH OF CIVILIZATIONS

The boy Jesus manifested extraordinary gifts and propensities. The spaces within his mind seemed so real and he experienced the uncanny ability to enter into it and to perform actions within it, much in the manner of what transpired in dreams, but which nevertheless produced real, visible, audible and tangible effects. What happened within him was translated as reality in space and time. Space and Time were as clay in his hands to be molded as he wished into the forms that he willed.

He learned that the Torah recounted the history of the Jewish people. The insistence on history made life to be considered as being linear with a beginning and an end. This factor gave a special significance to the passing moment as the gateway from here to eternity. For his civilization the Eternal was outside time. However, his associations with those he came into contact with while visiting the work yards of his father, showed him that there were others who thought that the Eternal lay hidden in the folds of time and was never outside it. They were those who believed in the circular nature of time with no beginning and no end, and that what goes around comes around. He lived in a civilization that thought that time was real, that forms were real. Yet he also knew there were others for whom time and space and everything inherently related to them were illusions, that there was no truth in them.

Even the thought process of his civilization was time bound. It was discursive and logical. It was argumentative. One idea led to another. It was a process that had a beginning and an end. This was the reasoning process. However, he knew that for other civilizations such processes were devoid of validity as regards religious truths. The religious goals were different for different civilizations. For some it was the Elysean Fields, for others eternity in Heaven, for yet others, it was the return of the disembodied soul to the One God in the sky. There were also those for whom it was the merger of the soul with the only true reality which was the divine consciousness, while for another multitude it was Enlightenment in this very life.

He knew and experienced them all because it was he in his body and spirit who was the source and fulfillment of them all since the foundation of the world. He was the WORD and the word was with God. There was nothing that was made or happened which was outside him or without him.

Gradually he realized a sense of a calling. If he had gifts that surpassed those of his contemporaries, was that in view of a mission to be conferred on him? Imbued with this thought he imagined himself as a vagabond preacher proclaiming to the world a new way, a new truth and a new life. What that really would be he still did not know. Yet his mind began to focus on future believers. Even if they thought that they had every reason to believe that his eventual teaching is substantially rooted in history, it would have a curious and fascinating relationship with myth and legend. History and myth were the pivots of all religious teachings. While history was confounded with reality, no such concession was made to myth. Yet it was myth the very ground of truth.

∽∽ ∽∽ ∽∽

CHAPTER 12 - FUNDAMENTAL QUESTIONS THAT AROSE

※※ ※※

So the question persisted. *What is truth?* Indeed the question had to be faced and answered. As his mind revolved around this issue, he was suddenly confronted with a strange scene. He saw himself hauled up before a judge in the attire of a Roman governor. That man was asking him a strange question: *What is truth?*

That question surprised him. How could this man who was a governor and a judge have accomplished his tasks without the faintest notion of what the *truth* was? Was it not ludicrous? Could there be realities which were far from being the truth but still direct the course of human destiny? So *what was truth?*

Then everything came alive within him. He saw the fanatical crowds. He saw the priests gloating in their victory over him. He felt the unendurable pain of the scourging, of the crowning with thorns. His body had been lacerated. His flesh was in shreds. His skin hung like worn out thread from his bloodied body. Everyone was shouting himself hoarse. The lust for blood and death was the driving force behind this tragedy. There was nothing that was still. Everything was moving, everything was changing. In this whirl and twirl of time only an enlightened mind would see the reality and the truth hidden within its folds.

He was now looking into the future. He saw scribes reveling in the art of describing what had taken place. They would pen the minutest of details of all those changing scenes. Scholars would pour over these writings perpetuating the names of the scribes and glorifying their deeds. They would refer to the literary forms those writers adopted and extol their ingenuity. Every conceivable rational argument would be directed to that end. But the truth would go unperceived and its bearer sent to his death, to his tomb, and presumably into oblivion.

Truth is a spiritual happening. It is individual. When an individual comes to that realization he goes beyond our grasp. An individual who has realized the truth experiences solitude and loneliness. He is alone, even when in the midst of millions. He is somewhere where the others are not. He cannot communicate with them. He tries but fails. He feels the failure. His only refuge, then becomes silence. This is what he experienced before the Roman governor. To the question: *what is truth*, his response was a deathlike silence. His truth was dead to them. Their reality was dead to him.

Now time and space had once again undergone a change within him. He was standing with a multitude as they pressed and squeezed one another making way for a funeral cortege. The bearers of the corpse were chanting: *only God is truth*. Long before his Roman judge was conceived and appeared on the scene, a people of a far away time and clime knew the answer to his question, that *Truth is God*. He still heard them chant as they bore the dead for cremation. *"For thousands of years they have come this way. All day and night"* bearing the dead on bamboo stretchers and passing through a final arch leading to the sacred river. There were among them the poorest of the poor. But so it was with the richest of the rich and the most powerful among the powerful. For one and all, from the humblest to the loftiest, there was only one truth, and that was God.

He realized that there is an outer reality, the one that passes, which is an illusion, and there is an innermost sense of reality which persists, which is truth. There is deep within us a sense of reality that identifies itself with TRUTH, with our personal truth. This reality is based on and has as its source the very human condition into which one is born. This truth is based on the fundamental questions arising from human existence, namely: where from, what and where to? It is based on our transient existence and the yearning for permanence and survival. It is based on the desire not to die and to live forever. It is the yearning for immortality.

When God brought the world into existence, God became the world which is the same as saying that the world became God. God ceased to remain above and beyond. He became the here and the now. God ceased to be in heaven. God put on the clothing of time and space. Time and space became the manifestations of God: God's revelation of Himself. God became the consciousness of the World. Divine consciousness became the only Reality and Truth of the world for only God is Truth.

If God being infinite, eternal and everlasting is the only reality and truth, then everything that is transient and that passes is non-reality and illusion. The still, silent and immovable presence, the source of all that exists is the only reality and truth. This is the only reason why the world of men is imbued, impregnated, and saturated with one and only concern, which is immortality. The word immortal is nothing but a synonym for God and hence the relentless unending yearning of man to make the world the gateway to life eternal.

CHAPTER 13 - GOD AND THE WORLD

One night Miriam dreamed a dream. Now it seemed to her that Jesus and she were living in another space and time. The location had changed and so had the circumstances. The flow of time has swept them away from the present. The whence and the whereto had no importance to them. What they were evoking now were common memories of bygone events.

Do you remember our meeting in the temple of Jerusalem? she was asking him. I saw you walking within those premises sunk in deep thought.

My memory was trying to rake up images from my past, he replied. I was trying to recall things bursting through the barriers of time.

But you were a little boy, she reminded him. What could your memory have stored so deep within you?

His reply caught her by surprise. *I was there from the beginning and so were you. The spirit of my Father was churning up remembrances from the ocean of my memory. Miriam*, he continued. *Do you remember, my mother took me to a soothsayer, a sage, and asked him to read my future.*

Yes I do, she answered, he said: *this boy has the making of a future vagabond preacher, living in a world of his own, a world of fantasies and dreams and visions, and who will introduce his followers to his own unique world. This 'out of this world' figure will incorporate within his person the beliefs widespread among the various communities that inhabited the cities and Mediterranean countries of our time. He will derive his strength from the wilderness that is the desert. He will delight in the high places the desert will offer him. But most of all he will derive his invincible inner power from the sacred feminine revealed to him as mother, lover and companion. His strange personality will give him the aurora of a God lost in the world of men. It could even well be that he is such a one.*

One thing the seer said stirred the depths of my heart: *but most of all he will derive his invincible inner power from the sacred feminine revealed to him as mother, lover and companion.*

Who would that be Jesus, that sacred feminine, who would that be? She asked.

His eyes were aglow while he listened to her. And now looking directly into her eyes he answered her question with the lines of sacred verse: *for my inward parts were woven me in the womb of our common mother, the mother Goddess that is Earth of which you Miriam are the eternal surrogate form.*

What he was now seeing was a vision emerging from a far away day in time. It was that of a statue representing mother and son, which millions were filing past. He approached the image and looked keenly at it. He saw a beautiful young woman across whose knees lay the dangling dead body of a young man.

How old is the man? he asked

Thirty three years, a passer by replied.

How did he die? he asked

He was sentenced to death by the priests of his own race, a sentence confirmed by the Roman governor of the province, and crucified.

And the woman, how old is she? He asked with great curiosity

About the same age I would say, the other replied.

Who is she? He asked

The dead man's mother, came the answer. The statue is called the *Pietà*

How can that be, she is a young woman, he said in astonishment. She is a very beautiful young woman, certainly a goddess. But who is she? She looks more a lover than a mother. Can one woman combine in her person both attributes of mother and lover?

The statue is called the *Pietà*, his interlocutor continued to explain. As for your last question, it may surprise you to know that the sculptor of this statue thought so. To clarify that conviction he carved out another statue with the images of the mother and lover on either side of the fallen man. Both women are embracing the dead body as if claiming it each as being her own. Also they both have the same name which further confirms his point of view. Then from the depths of his consciousness rose a voice which was saying: *the Father and I are One. Now it is I the eternal bridegroom. If the bridegroom and the Father are one, why cannot the bride and the Mother be One?*

The mystery of mother and lover now began to unravel within his mind. Since the greatest antiquity the earth goddess is depicted as carrying her first born male child. Also, since the greatest antiquity that male human being is portrayed as accompanied by two females, the duplications of the earth goddess herself as lover and mother. It is through the love relationship of mother earth with her male offspring that she realizes her role of motherhood.

Now his memory was churning up a well known scene. It was while the primordial man slept and dreamed a dream that the primordial woman arose out of that dream and took form. Out of the womb of the woman rose the man child. Out of the heart of that child become man rose the woman. The man child was alive in the womb of the woman, while the woman was alive in the heart of the man. Both were reciprocally the dream of the one and of the other. They were both finally the dream of the primordial womb, the mother goddess: the earth. It was she the ultimate mother, the ultimate lover, and the ultimate companion. Woman was her surrogate form: the mover of the cycle of human life with her threefold function.

They were now looking into each others eyes as if a common awareness had dawned on both. They were mutually conscious of what was transpiring in each other's mind.

Miriam he said, looking directly into her eyes. The forms that occupy the spaces of my mind are different, but not their identity. When I look at you I even experience a merging of forms into one woman who is all three: lover, mother and companion.

He did not hear her answer because memories were already filtering through his mind as he sat on the desert sands. His thoughts were conjuring up a scene, a scene with which he had become familiar through its countless repetitions. He closed his eyes, watched and listened as the scene was being re-enacted.

Miriam he said: listen. I hear your voice surging out of the depths of time. It is your voice though not your form that will reveal to me your identity. As if by an afterthought, he added: a day will come when you too will recognize me only by my voice and not by my form. He already saw himself standing by an open tomb and addressing a woman who was searching for him among the dead. He had called her by her name, and then only had recognition dawned in her mind.

The truth cannot get petrified in one human form, Jesus, Miriam was saying. Your attributes and your human experiences will determine the forms you will assume dictated by time and space. So too it will be with me. We will find our prolongations in surrogate forms and names. The one will become the many only because the many is really one. Therein is the role of history to provide the forms with which the divine can interact and use for its own manifestations.

CHAPTER 14 - GOD AND MAN

According to the Torah, God made him from the earth. But he was not made with the seed of man. He had no earthly father and no earthly mother as well, just as in his previous earthly appearance as the mysterious king of peace and high priest Melchizedek. His mother was mother earth. It was earth that God took in his hand and into which God breathed his image and likeness. No seed of man was involved in his creation, just earth in the hand of God and the divine breath. *What did that mean?* He wondered.

Then it dawned on him that his place of birth was the hand of God. It is there, and not to earth, that he would one day return. Then he heard the divine voice. God was telling him. *You did not arise directly from the earth, but from the earth held in my hand. It is out of my hand that you arose. When your day is over, it is into my hands you will return.*

The scene changed. What he was seeing now was a cross erected on the top of a mountain called Golgotha, and a man nailed to it. He saw himself dying, hanging on a cross and crying out *with a loud voice and saying: Father into thy hands I commit my spirit.* The breath of life that God infused into him was returning to the creator. As for his body, it will not see corruption as it was out of the hand of God he came to be. He recalled in this connection words uttered about a holy one whose body God will not allow to decay.

So too it was with Eve, who was formed from his own body that rose out of the hand of God. Her spirit too would return to the hand of God and she too would not see corruption. Her body arose out of a body that came directly from the hand of God. Her future rebirths would be through immaculate conceptions. Full realization now dawned on him that he and the woman sprang from the same source, to which they would also return. Their source of origin and final destination were the same. They were bound together by one common destiny for all eternity. In fact their union from the very beginning was eternal. As the direct, untainted image and likeness of God. They were since their origin and like their source, infinite, eternal and everlasting.

He the primordial man and she the primordial woman were made of uncontaminated virgin earth held in the hand of God. But not so their descendants. Their progeny would be born of their seed and flesh, but in another dispensation which was that of time and space. It was a dispensation in which everything was destined to be born and to die. That dispensation would be a passing scene such as a stage set up wherein actors would appear and disappear sporting masks of temporary identities. Furthermore, within that new dispensation lurked the danger of an evil entity as slithery, slippery and seductive as a serpent, a force that would be lurking in the undergrowth of their consciousness.

Adam and Eve knew that someone or other from among their children would succumb to a temptation which would change the destiny of all. So they made themselves vicariously liable by assuming that guilt. Their act of yielding to the tempter was not disobedience to God, but an act of solidarity with his creation. Their intention was to share the destiny of their erring descendants, leading them through the labyrinthine ways of their minds to the light of the divine consciousness hidden within them.

Now ever since the episode of the tree of good and evil things had changed. The evil that had been hidden from their perspectives had now taken root in the minds of their descendants. The hand of God being withdrawn from under their feet, they were in the throes of a free fall from light to darkness, from wisdom to ignorance. They were now as it were in a cave looking at the shadows the light from outside was projecting on the cave walls all around them and taking them for reality. They were now in a world of time and space, in a world of illusions. They were now in a world where everything passed as in a dream. Even the dreamer was one such passing phenomenon and therefore himself a dream.

He and his spouse had heard the divine declaration: *Dust you are and unto dust you shall return.* But that decree did not affect them. They had been born out of the hand of God and not directly of the earth. So that curse would not influence their destiny but that of their progeny. Furthermore God who knows all things and knows the heart of man knew of their sacrifice and their intent. As for the primordial man and the primordial woman they voluntarily entered the realm of the quicksand that is time and space with the sole intent of sharing the destiny of their progeny and to ensure their redemption. God's loving care would guide and follow them.

They already had proof of God's tenderness in their regard. Seeing their nakedness and shame God had himself even made them clothes of skin and promised a redeemer for fallen mankind. That Redeemer would be called the son of man. That was he, Jesus, who as Adam had been the primordial man called by the same name. He would be born of virgin earth just as the bare earth in the hand of God from which he had risen. That Redeemer would bear the same image and likeness as that which God had imparted to him, to Adam.

Adam and Eve would not experience corruption being reduced to dust after death, but would return to fulfill their mission of being with their progeny until the end of the earth. Their identity would fuse and merge with that of the Messiah himself. Their mission of salvation would endure until the end of time.

As for their progeny God had removed from under them his supporting hand. So they became earth bound, with the gravity of flesh, drawing them to the earth and finally to its dust.

CHAPTER 15 - MAN AND WOMAN

He recalled how he had told a gathering regarding the relationship between the first man and his spouse: *She is now flesh of my flesh and bone of my bone; She shall be called Woman, Because she was taken out of Man.* For this reason a man shall leave his father and his mother, and be joined to his wife; and they shall become one flesh. *So they are no longer two, but one flesh. What therefore God has joined together, let no man separate.* But then their condition had undergone a change. What no man could separate the new reality of death was now able to do. So the bond between man and woman was modified by a new clause: *till death do us apart.*

Then a voice surged from within him. It was telling him, you are not subject to death. You are the divine word. You are the eternal 'logos'.

And she? He asked, anxious for her personal survival.

Do not feel apprehensive, the same voice told him. She is wisdom, the eternal Sophia. She is your very substance, for what is the word without wisdom? The eternal word and the eternal wisdom of God that you are, nothing can do you apart. You are not only one flesh, but one spirit and one consciousness which is divine.

But we are now in another dispensation being that of time and space. Our physical forms are subject to death, he argued.

You are one consciousness the voice insisted. You will together witness your coming in and going out. You will never cross the river of oblivion: the Lethe or the Vaitarna or any other that divides and separates.

You will never cross the river of oblivion: the Lethe or the Vaitarna were the words now reverberating in his mind. Yes my baba, said a woman's voice interrupting his thoughts. I will never let you depart from my life

As now he was reliving an episode from his past. How many times had he died and been revived by this woman, this very same woman. He saw himself in a flash bodyless on the banks of the river Vaitarna looking out for a boat with a ferryman to take him across to the smoke filled ethereal everlasting shores of Vaikuntha. Then he saw the dark shadow of an old wooden ferryboat looming on the edge of the bank without any boatman in sight. Emaciated as he was he doubted his ability to ferry his boat to the other shore. But something puzzled him. How did he get to the banks of the Vaitarna without passing over the pyre? He strained his mind trying to remember and then the semblance of a recollection returned to him. He was witnessing his funeral pyre blazing against the dark mist covered sky. Who is doing all this? He had asked himself because he saw his pyre unattended. Who lit it, he asked?

Then he recalled a faint voice that of a woman answer. He strained his ears and barely captured the words she uttered but he heard her say: *I.*

He had fixed his eyes in the direction from which the voice emanated. As he got used to the eerie darkness he had seen a womanly silhouette covered in white that barely distinguished her from the smoke filled surrounding. He saw her seated besides the pyre quietly stirring it and watching it being reduced to ashes. He watched the swirling grey ash flakes disperse until nothing remained. Deep stillness suffused his being invaded by the thought that all his connections, yearnings, joys and heartaches had vanished into nothingness. *This was all there was to it*, he had murmured to himself.

The stillness had expanded and seemed to hold eternity in its embrace. Suddenly he had heard the rustling of a woman's dress near to him. The same rustling sound he had heard what seemed an eternity ago as his body lay on a cold stone slab in a burial vault near the Golgotha hill. As he got used to the ghostly happenings he saw the same womanly silhouette. Who are you? he asked. In answer to his question the figure had slowly removed the veil from her face and in one instant recognition had dawned: Maya, he shouted, Maya, it is you.

Yes me, replied the figure of the woman. What is there in a name or even a form, It is the identity that matters. I followed you my Baba. I never left your side. I followed you over the years, and everywhere you went. I saw your body on the banks of mother Ganga with no one to attend to you. It was I who made the pyre and placed you on it. I lit the pyre and am watching as the flames rise towards the sky taking you along with them. Baba, my Baba, I cried the day you left me, I cried as I followed you over the arid desert, its plains and hills during your wanderings. I cried when I saw you seated alone on the banks of the sacred river, alone, yes alone. And now I cry as I see you trying to ferry yourself across the Vaitarna, the waters of the great divide from where there is no return.

I will not let you go alone my Baba. I would gladly follow you to where you go, but my time has not yet come. Come back my Baba, come back, to me. She was holding out her hand towards him in a pleading tone that melted his heart.

Maya he had cried. I am coming back to you my love, I am coming back. As he spoke he saw the whitish lumpings of ash strewn on the site of his pyre levitating in a terrifying whirl and re-assuming his physical form.

His consciousness had been turned into an ocean in storm. How long it took to subside he did not remember, but when it finally did he heard the voice say: you will continuously seek each other, being drawn to each other by the magnetism of the spirit, and you will always find each other though hell should bar the way.

* * * * *

His mind was now turning over the pages of their lives. He was facing the tree of good and evil, the serpent and the apple. They had succumbed only apparently to the devil's temptation. Their apparent consent was through their sense of solidarity with their progeny. Their liability and punishment was vicarious. They were submitting to it voluntarily. So too it was with their deaths and separation. It was voluntary, but yet it was painful and anguishing.

What he saw now was the apple which the serpent was offering them. What was really that apple? He wondered. That fruit was the embodiment of earthly desire, of greed and lust. It was the call to experience the pleasures of the flesh. It was the apple that Paris gave to Venus for her promise of the possession of the most beautiful woman of the world. That choice launched war and destruction. It marked the beginning of separation and the uncertain danger filled return home.

Indeed the perspectives had now changed. Greed and Lust had entered the lives of mankind and with it the feeling of shame at their nakedness. Lust and pleasure had plunged them into darkness and ignorance the new overlords of the human destiny. The new dispensation would be that of the blind leading the blind through labyrinthine ways without issue, veritable paths to nowhere inscribed in their minds and hearts. Only he and his consort could change the tide. There was no question about it. They had to be there together until the end of time.

CHAPTER 16 - SATAN DECEIVED

✖︎✖︎ ✖︎✖︎

Now he was experiencing the stirrings of the spirit within him. It moved his form within its inner spaces as if called by a distant voice: the distant but familiar voice of a woman.

Eve, he said, *where are you? Have our paths bifurcated? Has each one of us gone his own way? Have you left me to experience my loneliness and solitude?*

He was now walking followed by a big crowd. He walked over the sandy paths and through populated villages amidst mud and stone-constructed dwellings. The people lined the roads to see him pass through. Then of a sudden he heard a woman scream. He heard his name being uttered in a loud and frenzied manner. No one else heard it but he. His eyes probed the corners of the streets before he began treading resolutely in a certain direction, the direction in which his spirit was leading him. The shouts were now getting louder and louder until a door burst open and a woman thrust herself into his view. What he saw resembled an apparition. It was a woman held tight within the coils of seven serpents. He recognized the woman and the serpent who held her in his grip.

You needed seven of your forms to immobilize her, he said.

Yes, I had to use all my might, was the answer.

Why so?

Can you not remember, Adam, the serpent was asking. I used only one form to bend her to my will.

Did you really? He asked.

Of course. That was my greatest victory. I thrust you from wisdom to ignorance, from light to darkness where you and yours are still groping in search of the absent light. I pulled you away from doing his will, and made you do yours which is finally none other than mine.

I would not think so Lucifer, he answered quietly. It was the woman and her mate who won the encounter. We deceived the deceiver. We took that stand to ensure that our progeny would not be alone, for behold, we are with them till the end of time. Wisdom and light will be the ultimate winners. The day will come when only God's will will be done.

Then he approached the woman and addressed the writhing demons. *I exorcise you, depart from this woman and never approach her again.*

With terrible hissing sounds and frightening writhing and contortions the seven serpents unwound themselves and glided away into the desert. The woman ran forward to him, fell at his feet and embraced his legs holding fast to him. His mind was now racing forward in time. He saw himself at an open tomb and a woman, this same woman addressing him, requesting a man she thought was the gardener to be told about the body of her lord that had gone missing.

Tell me where you have placed him, Sir, so that I could go and bring him back.

She was now confronted by flashbacks claiming the place of the present moment. She was asking the gardener of another location to be told where she would find the body of her other half who would wake up from his slumber on hearing her approach. On waking up he had addressed her by her name and said: Eve. Transpiring at this very moment was a scene that seemed to duplicate one of the flashbacks she had just confronted.

And now he spoke to her and said: *Mary*.

At that moment she recognized him, ran to him, fell at his feet and embraced his legs clinging to him as she was doing now.

As that vision faded, he told her: eons have gone by since we first met, or have they? Or is it the wheel of time that seems to turn while remaining still forever? Nothing has changed, just our forms. Nothing has changed just the surroundings and the relationships.

During all these eons I searched for you in all the highways and the byways of life. Searched for you relentlessly moved by the unfailing conviction that I will find you though hell itself should bar the way, she answered.

When he glanced back towards his disciples and the crowd, he saw them standing in sheer amazement. Some of them were already running in all directions bearing the news. The master had delivered a woman of seven devils. Soon stories began to spread about the woman. She was young and rich. Now she was following him, standing just behind him, attentive to everything he said and to every need of his, be it the most simple. Mary of Magdala, they said to one another, Mary of Magdala.

The news also spread that the master felt himself particularly attached to her and often spoke to her in isolation when the day was over and she lay seated at his feet. They dared not approach them as they were together, but suspected that they conversed about truths hidden from their minds, secrets of which they did not have direct experience. Some of them had even heard her refer to the master as Adam, and the news spread that he was Adam reborn among them.

What was time, what was space for the divine consciousness? Within what is eternally still, the wheel of time turns only in appearance. One who understands the nature of the mirage does not rush to drink from its springs. He knows it for what it is, a pure illusion that he was seeing and experiencing. No illusion can fill hunger and thirst. They recalled him telling another woman who had come to draw at a well: *the water you draw will never quench your thirst. But the waters I shall give you are the waters of eternal life. Once you drink of it your thirst will be quenched for ever.*

CHAPTER 17 - DOUBTS THAT APPEAR

But the waters I shall give you are the waters of eternal life. Once you drink of it your thirst will be quenched for ever.

Which water are you thinking about? a well known voice asked him. *There was once water that filled numerous jugs. But when, on your order they were drawn out, that water had turned into wine. Offering water is an occupation for mortals. You must decide who you are Jesus, mortal or divine. If you are divine you cannot be satisfied with offering water. You will feel obliged not only to turn that water into wine, but eventually that wine into your blood. Jesus, you have to decide. Do it now.*

Am I human or divine? If I am human then am I not wasting my years and my youth with the useless dreams of a deluded mind. Assailed by these questions and overcome by fatigue, he soon fell asleep. It was then that he felt the rustle of a woman's clothing by his side. He dreamed that his mother was inviting him to accompany her to a wedding feast. He felt happy. There he would be a man among men and women. He would enjoy. He would eat and drink, and dance as well. The sleeper stirred as he and his mother entered the wedding hall.

And so they enjoyed. The music was blaring away tunes punctuated by drum beats while the dancing girls swayed to and fro rhythmically. The guests seated at the tables engaged in friendly conversations and pleasantries. The newly weds seated on a dais under an archway of flowers received the wishes of all the invitees. Hectic activity was seen at the back of the house where family members, relatives and close friends prepared and served refreshing drinks and steaming dishes. The males saw to it that the flow of wine did not abate. Mary and her son mingled with the guests, many of whom were known to them. Jesus had left all his pressing thoughts and concerns behind him and took part in the rejoicing with gay abandon. He for once felt being a man among men, a human being among others.

And then what happened was like a thunderbolt from the blues. News reached them from the deliverers of wine that their stocks had run out and that no more wine would be available for the wedding feast. The feast was in full swing and it was the wine that maintained the gaiety at the highest level. The unforeseen situation would not only dull the proceedings, but would also generate discontent among the guests and bring the family to disrepute and ridicule. The women folk of the family, close friends of Mary, discretely brought this to her attention as well as their concern for the humiliation which would afflict the family. The resultant situation would also not be of a good augur for the newly weds. Instinctively Mary looked around for her son with whom to share her heavy heart.

He had joined the guests on the dance floor and was totally absorbed in the music, the drum beats and the enlivening rhythms. Mary kept watching her son until for a fleeting moment their eyes met. That was sufficient to tell Jesus that all was not well with his mother. He interrupted his merriment and quietly made his way towards her. What he heard and all its implications struck him forcefully, but he felt hard put to shake off his determination of enjoying the day. Yet that enjoyment itself would be affected by the prevailing situation. And so in spite of a feeble remonstrance to his mother that his moment had not yet come, he pondered his next move. That next move was precipitated by his mother's voice telling the servers to do as her son told them. They had now turned towards him awaiting his instructions.

Yet his thoughts were elsewhere. In the spaces that opened before him he saw a group of disciples. Their faces too were turned towards him in the expectancy of a discourse. He heard himself tell them: *I am the vine, you are the branches; he who abides in Me and I in him, he bears much fruit.*

Then he heard a voice which told him: *indeed you are the vine. Now what does the vine yield but 'wine'. The vine absorbs the water from the earth and transforms it into wine. Now this is what you are about to do, change water into wine.*

Fill the jugs with water, he told the servers.

They filled them to the brim. It all happened in a short interval, but it seemed to him to be much drawn out than it appeared. The flow of time had stopped and his form seemed engulfed in a vacuum. The earth that made up his form seemed formless and empty. His spirit had left his body and was now moving over the waters. And then he saw himself hanging from the cross in the throes of an excruciatingly agonizing death. He felt a spear pierce his side and from it blood and water flowed. The voice he had heard before was making itself heard again.

You are the vine. The water you draw is within you, you turn it into 'wine'. But Transforming that wine into blood is beyond the scope of the vine. Such a task, Jesus, is Divine.

The blood that was flowing from his side had collected into a chalice he held in his hands. This scene had suddenly come alive in his spirit. What he beheld were disciples seated around the table of the last supper and he was offering them his blood in the guise of wine. *Take this and drink of it, for this is my blood,* he had told them. With those words he had passed the cup of wine become blood around the table. Once the chalice had been emptied of its content, he was saying: do this in remembrance of me. When you remember who I am, then will you also remember who you are, for I and you are ONE and the SAME: the same body and the same blood. We are THAT.

As the scene faded away he saw the servers standing before him in great expectancy. What he felt now was a breath-taking experience. His whole body suddenly become taut and stretched to the four corners of the earth had taken a vegetal form heavily laden with clusters of ripe fruit. Their juice was ooozing out of the bursting fruit and pouring into jugs placed under them just as the blood from his pierced heart had dripped into the chalice. As he remained stunned by this strange occurrence he heard the mysterious voice making itself heard again: you are the vine. The water you draw is within you. The fruit you bear in such profusion is now being churned into 'wine'. When the voice ceased so did the transformation.

Still in the throes of the mysterious happening he told the servers: *draw from the jugs and hand me a cup of wine.* They did as he told them. It was now the chalice that contained his blood that he was holding in his hands He drank of it and said: *draw from the jugs and pass the cups around. Let them all drink of it.* What he was seeing was the chalice with his blood which was being transferred from one set of hands to another. And so wine flowed once more. This is fresh new wine, he heard the master of ceremonies tell his staff. Why did you serve it last?

Emerging from his vision and quickened by the new wine he strode back to the dance floor where everyone continued to revel. Very soon his feet were tripping on the ground with arms flaying the air while he emitted the sounds produced by the other dancers. Then when he woke up with a jerk his dream was gone. What lay before him was the great wasteland that was the desert. Once again he was alone. Fully immersed in the dream that had just unfolded within him, he went to sleep again.

∽∽ ∽∽ ∽∽

CHAPTER 18 - HUMAN OR DIVINE

Once again, much as tried to subdue them, he was hearing voices rising from within him and vying for recognition. His attention was caught by a particular voice. This particular voice was telling him:

Jesus, you must decide. Are you human or divine? You cannot live both lives simultaneously. You are one or the other. Try again and make your definitive choice.

Am I a human being or divine? This was the question he now had to answer.

What are the criteria that make a being human or divine? He was now hearing a distraught woman addressing words of reproach to him.

She was saying: *Your father and I have been anxiously searching for you.*

He saw himself stretching his hands towards his disciples and replying: *Behold my mother and my brothers! For whoever does the will of my Father who is in heaven, he is my brother and sister and mother.*

Now what was the will of his Father in heaven in his regard? His earthly mother and father had related to him their dreams that led to his birth. Those narratives were not easy for him to fathom. Although he was dealing with dreams, they nevertheless raised doubts in him as to his physical origin. His birth had in no way been a normal human birth. Going by his earthly parents' declarations, he was partly divine and partly human, or wholly divine or wholly human or even wholly divine and wholly human. Could he be wholly the one and the other? The truth as it seemed to him was that God had provided the male seed for his conception, while a woman, his mother, had accepted its implantation in her womb.

He recalled the episode described in the Torah where God took a lump of earth in his hand and breathed into it his divine breath. Thus had arisen the first man, the primordial man. It appeared to him that his own birth was modeled on the lines of that of the primordial man. God had taken a lump of earth in its surrogate form of woman, and breathed into it his spirit. That was the will of his Father. The reply he had given to the distraught woman was exactly that which the primordial man Adam would have addressed to her. His origin his existence, and his mission, had only one source – the will of God. Just as was his birth, so too would also be his death. It would be summed up by the words: *not my will but Thine be done.*

As this truth erupted into his consciousness bursting forth from abysmal depths, he heard himself declare loud and clear: *For this I have been born, and for this I have come into the world.* Yet the singularity of his condition would not give him the respite he sought. His mind continued to be borne on turbulent waves of thoughts. Was I born into a body to forsake its physical pleasures? The question persisted. How could that be the will of my Father?

He was shaken from his reverie by the speaker who was pointing out to empty jugs aligned against the walls of a kitchen. You did it once for others. Now do it for yourself. Have them filled with water and turn it into wine. Once again a great thirst took possession of him. Go, the tempter was telling him, go do it, for you are my beloved son in whom I am well pleased. The voice even seemed to descend from heaven. Go, the voice repeated, please yourself, have your pleasure, love your human life to the hilt, for only then will I be pleased with you.

He was now turning to the stewards once again and telling them: fill the jugs with water. Now draw and bring it to me.

He heard a voice say: do as the bridegroom says. Take all the mugs to him, they are his.

Bridegroom? he asked in wonderment, bridegroom?

Why not? the voice replied. Do you not see you are in a bridal chamber? It is the duty of the bridegroom to provide the wine. Then he recalled the word he would utter one day: *Can the children of the bridal chamber fast, while the bridegroom is with them? As long as they have the bridegroom with them, they cannot fast.* Only then did realization dawn on him that it was he the bridegroom. It was he, for he had been draped in all the finery of a bridegroom. He was now seeing himself in his previous forms as bridegroom, as Adam wooing Eve with the words: you are flesh of my flesh and blood of my blood. Then he saw the wooing and wedding of Rebecca, the sacred idyll of Ruth and Boaz. It was all happening, and happening in Cana of Galilee. He glanced sideways and saw the radiant bride. For a moment he felt stunned to silence.

You? he asked in a state of great bewilderment.

Who else could it be, my love, but me, she answered softly. We are here to enjoy our youthful lives.

He was now dazed and enraptured by her beauty. The words of the song of Solomon gushed out from his lips: *Your breasts are perfectly formed like goblets filled with mixed wine.* He was now holding two goblets in his hands and drinking out of both at once. He went on drinking because they were always full. And so he drank and drank. Now staring at her with drunken dreamy eyes, he ordered her: dance.

The scene changed once more. The wedding garb he was wearing had now mysteriously changed into regal clothes. He was seated on a throne surrounded by adoring subjects. The order he had given made itself heard once more: dance, he was repeating. And the woman danced. It was salacious and sexual; alluring and, lustful. Never would he have imagined that the female body could assume such seductive postures. *It is the dance of the seven veils, he* heard someone in the assembly say. The dance of the seven veils, he repeated to himself and that rang a well known chord in his ears, but so drunk he was he could no longer remember. He watched the woman enthralled as she gracefully and rhythmically whirled and gyrated lasciviously with consummate ease, an incarnation of the very spirit of physical decadence. In one hand she held a lotus blossom, the scepter of Isis, and the sacred flower of Egypt and India, while in the other she held a phallic emblem, the token of the sacrifice of her virginity to him.

Then the voice within him made itself manifest again: go, it said, join her. She is offering her virginity to you. Take it, it is now or never. You are the spirit, she is the eternal waters.

Out of the depths of his memory arose the form of Miriam, who had saved him from the waters of the Nile and other Israelite women dancing and singing after their escape from the Egyptians. Merging with this scene was that of the golden calf and the women who were dancing frenetically around it. Deeply affected by that scene, he instinctively refused to do that bidding.

You are wrong said the voice. There is no golden calf here. You will realize who you are when you join her.

And so he launched himself on the floor amidst wild clapping and hysterical womanly shrieks. The shrieks became wilder and increasingly more frenzied as he took the woman in his arms and responded to each and every movement of her luscious body. She had now shed her veils as he had done with his clothes. They were revealing themselves in all their nudity and they felt no shame. This is paradise, this is paradise they shouted in sheer exultation, we are naked with no feeling of shame. Adam and Eve they were, inebriated with the wine calling them to life and in the throes of ecstatic delight.

Then the scene changed again. He saw himself accompanying a cortege of revelers who were carrying the ark of the covenant to the temple. Leaning towards his bride he whispered: you are the ark of the new covenant between God and man. She sensed the change and felt him undergo a transformation.

Suddenly turning to him she asked: *who are you?*

He did not have to answer because the air was rent with the tumultuous sound of a clamouring crowd. They were shouting his name. David, the voices said, David. He was now holding the ark of the Lord now manifested in a womanly form in his arms. He was leaping unbridled and uninhibited and bereft of all his clothing. From above, from what seemed to be a balcony window words uttered by another woman reached him. She said: You, king of Israel, are you not ashamed dancing uncovered before your handmaids? Whose were these voices he wondered. Who was she who uttered them: lover, mother or companion?

Now the fumes of the wine he had imbibed were subsiding within him and the scene was vanishing from his view. He was brought to his senses by the loud guffaws of vulgar laughter. *Follow me, Jesus,* that voice was saying, *and I will give you this world, the world that you saw and experienced, for your unique enjoyment for time without end. You are a man. Do not let your dream of divinity destroy your humanity.*

When he opened his eyes, he was not alone. *I was there with you* she said. *We were naked and we were dancing. I was there with you and I danced as Miriam did when we escaped the clutches of the Egyptians. I was dancing with you when you called me the ark of the new covenant between you and God. You told me: a*nd I saw the holy city, new Jerusalem, coming down out of heaven from God, made ready as a bride adorned for her husband. And I heard a loud voice from the throne, saying, "Behold, the tabernacle of God is among men, and He will dwell among them. Yes. Jesus, you told me that I was the tabernacle of God among men. *You are not only a king but also a priest. You and I we are priest and priestess of the mother Goddess. Jesus, we know of no other god but her. She is your lover, your mother and your companion, all three in one person.* She is the ark of the covenant, the new covenant between God and man, the tabernacle of God among men. Jesus, That is I. I am the divine Trinity, the three persons in one physical form."

As she spoke the woman in his arms was undergoing a metamorphosis. Slowly but surely her form was changing. She was assuming a roundish shape that became smaller and smaller and finally assumed the shape of a fruit: a fruit that was an apple. As he stood hypnotized by what was occurring before his eyes, he distinctly saw the fruit being held in the mouth of a serpent which was dangling from a tree. Now the serpent was beckoning to him.

Adam, renounce to your earlier commitment. In that first garden this fruit was the symbol of greed and lust. Now you have seen it take form for what it really is. It is for this form that the sons of god, the angels have lusted and descended from heaven to have their fill of earthly pleasure. Adam you too are a son of God. Indulge in the pleasures this form is offering you in such abundance. That form was more intoxicating than wine and more luscious than apples. May I quote to your from your scriptures: *'Oh, may your breasts be like clusters of the vine, and the scent of your breath like apples.'*

But now the spirit of God was with him and his composure had returned. He told the serpent: what you saw was an illusion, a drama on the passing stage of time and devoid of content or substance.

Adam the serpent said. You ate of the apple. You enjoyed the physical form that apple took. You enjoyed the taste of the fruit. You enjoyed the pleasure of the form the fruit assumed. Now there is one last chance I am offering to you to realize and enjoy the happiness your human form can afford you.

CHAPTER 19 - TEMPTATIONS INTENSIFY

✘✘ ✘✘

The scene was now fading while the serpent put him once again in a state of a deep trance. Seeing the far away look in his eyes the serpent now changed tactics. He assumed the form of a beautiful, seductive woman and danced. But on this occasion too, the spirit wrought a profound change within Jesus. It was all happening elsewhere than where he first was. He saw himself clothed differently seated once again under a tree with flying buttress roots. It was the tree under which a woman had placed bowls of food and drink for him.

His mind was in the state of a profound stillness as he searched to unite with the consciousness deep within him. He had the feeling of being drawn down into the ocean depths where all was silent and still. His thoughts had come to a standstill just as the identities they generated. He was feeling the overwhelming stillness and silence of a deep sleep out of which only the dream of the ineffable could emerge. He had realized this state when the serpent metamorphosed into the form of a woman danced before him in an unrestrained and frenzied manner, swirling and twirling until her clothes were in tatters and lay in shreds at her feet. Her voluptuous body was now glistening being bathed in her perspiration, but she danced on with ever renewed energy. Her dance would have enticed, delighted and seduced all the pagan gods of Imperial Egypt, Greece and Rome, but the one main spectator of the scene remained stoic and impassive.

While the woman danced and he seemingly watched, his imagination was conjuring before him scene after scene of the sacred scriptures, of beautiful and lustful women who used their seductive powers for personal, economic or political gain. What appeared before him was flesh and blood and not phantasms. He watched in total impassivity as one and all offered their bodies to him as bait for more than what the riches and the kingdoms of the universe could offer. Among them was Delilah, who tore from Samson the secret of his incomparable physical prowess. He saw Salome shedding her seven veils before Herod and claiming as her prize the head of the Baptist.

Then there came Jezebel whose gorgeous body was torn to bits and devoured by dogs. And so the scenes eclipsed one another. Now it was the turn of Herodias whose incestuous union with Herod Antipas called for the wrath of the Baptist, and Potiphar's wife whose wiles sent Joseph into exile in Egypt. Then the scenes of Lot's daughters copulating with their old father unfurled before him. He had seen them all as in a theater on the stage that was the mirage of time. All he felt for these unfortunate women was love, sympathy and compassion.

He still remained unawakened from what seemed an age long reverie while the voice of the woman now occupied the scene.

See Adam, I am Salome, it is I who danced before Herod, such a voluptuous, sensual, lascivious and seductive dance that it merited for me the head of your baptizer, John. Look at me Jesus, watch me dance. I do not want any heads, Jesus, it is you I want. I will give you love Jesus, a woman's love that no riches and no kingdoms can buy.

But the person to whom she addressed his words did not hear her anymore. He was deep within himself looking on without the least twitch of his body betraying the least emotion. Seeing that his attempts were futile the angel of death left him. Jesus came out of his trance and saw that he was alone.

I am leaving you for a while said the devil, but you are not yet done with me. I will be back with the offer of a final chance for you, Adam. Adam, on that day you will be put to the ultimate test

What is it and when and where will that be? He asked.

That will be the day you will be risen again from your deep sleep on the cross. No one will expect your resurrection, no one, not even the flesh of your flesh and bone of your bone, Miriam. She will come to the tomb laden with perfumes and spices to anoint you for your definitive burial. Even the empty tomb will not arouse the least suspicion of a resurrection. Her question to the supposed gardener will be for information as to the location of your body, so that she could bring it back to its proper resting place. Your disciples would be in hiding through sheer fear of being identified as believers in you.

Jesus, it will be a woman's voice that will wake you. It is also by your voice that she will recognize you. The disciples on their way to Emmaus thought they had recognized you by an act you had performed, that of breaking bread. Peter and others fishing in the high seas saw you approaching them walking on the waves and took panic assuming the figure to be a phantom. Thomas saw you in close proximity along with the others, and still doubted that it was you. The only feature that evoked knowledge of you were the wounds that he touched. It was not the physical form but other features such as the voice, the touch and also an act performed such as the breaking of bread that caused recognition of you. Your physical form always remained elusive. Indeed if their minds had no reasons to recognize you, how could sensations be conclusive in that regard? It is one or other of such hidden traits that will lead to your identification. Without such manifestations you will go incognito.

You would live your life as anyone else, if not for such sudden recollections you evoke in others. That will be your greatest temptation Adam, the temptation to cut the rope of what you consider to be your divine mission with its total irremediable failure on earth, and to live your human life drinking from *'breasts like clusters of the vine, and bathing in the scent of forms with breath like apples.'* You will be thirty three years of age Jesus and the weight of youth will be heavily on your side. Decide wisely Jesus and live the rest of your long life happily on earth, in a land of your choice. Or else….

Or else what, Satan?

Or else you will be haunted by the lament of the children sitting in the market place, crying out: *We played the pipe for you but you did not dance.*

Satan, he said, my mission is to proclaim immortal life to all who believe in me.

Immortal life, immortal life, the serpent sneered. If deluded mankind is determined to crucify someone to achieve immortal life they will do so, be it you or another. And if it wants to resurrect you from your tomb to achieve the same end, it will do it too. Just look around you and see the numerous temples of saviour gods who died and were resurrected. You will end up as one of them. You are only a paper hero come alive: the hero of a bunch of parchments called the sacred scriptures written by dreamers and visionaries as well as tricksters and fraudsters.

Jesus, these are my parting words. Come out of your mind. Cease to be a figment of your imagination. Your prayer that the will of your father in heaven be done on earth as it is in heaven is doomed to total failure. You will go down in history as a fantasy figure, a Don Quixote, a bait a new class of priests will not cease to tender to gullible believers with a view to establishing their own kingdom, their own power, and their own glory. The truth they will arrogate to themselves will not be your truth, but their own, their own concoctions, the product of their own minds. Jesus, there will come a day when a religion imposed on an empire will have its origin in the vision of a mundane pagan emperor, and your identity will be determined by Imperial Decree.

CHAPTER 20 - GOD'S IDENTITY BY IMPERIAL DECREE

The last sentence uttered by Satan struck him with the force of thunder. What he was now seeing was a Roman general leading his troops to battle suddenly dazzled by the sight of a cross in the sky with a halo composed of the words: *with this sign you will be victorious*. Was that vision real? Was it an illusion? Was it a trick? Was it a fraud? No one will ever know.

The scene had now changed and he saw the same emperor imposing a strange unintelligible definition of his identity and person. This definition composed of lofty specious words engendering void and empty thoughts like paths that led to nowhere, were enforced on a subservient group of strangely clad individuals for unconditional acceptance. It would be this imperial decree, the belief or non-belief in which, that would determine both life and death on earth, as well as life eternal for all mankind, be it in heaven or in hell.

The devil had now wafted him to the summit of a mountain from which he saw displayed the believers of the religion supposedly founded by him. It was a religion of no compromise. The God of that religion was portrayed as one with a welcome board in one hand, and a bloody sword in the other. The wording on the board read: believe and enter, OR ELSE…the arrow that followed the last words were pointing to the sword.

Is this the God you call your father? The devil was asking him.

I have nothing to do with beliefs, he answered. My conviction is based on knowledge that erupted within me through my 'Awakening'. The stilleness that followed was impregnated with the Awareness, the Divine consciousness, that 'I am God'. That same spirit is in labour within each and everyone with all enduring birth pains until that same awareness dawns in all.

It is the Spirit that is divine consciousness that leads us to the light from the darkness. One does not have to drink the whole ocean water to know its salty taste. A drop of the infinite and eternal ocean of divine consciousness within each is all that one needs to arrive at such an awareness. That ocean is contained in its drop. That ocean has flowed into that drop.

And so he remained untouched, unmoved and adamant. I will not go against the will of God, he said. The mind and the will of man in my regard is of no concern to me and to those who seek the truth within themselves. The kingdom I preach is nowhere outside and is not of this earth. He would make this declaration in no uncertain terms before a jury of religious judges even when his very earthly existence was at stake. That kingdom he preached is within each and every one.

Then what arose before him took him completely by surprise. It was Eve. *Think well she reminded him. The will of God cannot take you away from me. We are one flesh. We cannot tear ourselves asunder by each following a different path. What one decides and does the other too must decide and do. Do not forget, indeed never forget that no garden of delights can ever offer you the delights that I offer you. I am your garden of delights. As long as I am with you, you will have your delights without end.*

Adam, can you remember why God made me? Because he knew that you were alone. He said: it is not good for man to be alone. God does not want us to know evil. The greatest evil in the life of a man is being alone. It is solitude. I tell you, hell is solitude. It is to save you from the greatest evil, that of solitude that could befall a man that God made me out of you. As long as I am with you you will not see evil. Even if you are in the shadow of darkness and in the valley of death you will not fear evil as long as I am with you.

Believe me, you are now more important to me than God himself. Remember what God our father told us at the beginning of our creation. God made them male and female. For this reason a man shall leave his father and mother and be joined to his wife, and the two shall become one flesh. So they are no longer two, but one flesh. Therefore what God has joined together, let no one separate. I repeat, a man shall leave his father and mother and be joined to his wife, and the two shall become one flesh. So they are no longer two, but one flesh. Who is now our father? It is God. Who is our mother? It is God. It is his commandment, that you leave him and be joined to me for ever.

Jesus, the voice of the serpent now took over. Use your eventual rebirth that you call your resurrection and benefit by your anonymity to flee the scene and live the full life that I have offered you. Leave this land and go into a distant realm, disappear into the masses so that not even your heavenly father could rediscover you.

Jesus, you know the will of that father, your loving father whose only begotten son you are, in your regard. It is that you should die. Consider this Jesus, how could such a father will that you die on behalf of humanity created from NOTHING? How could a father, an eternally, infinitely loving father sacrifice his only son for a mere NOTHING? What kind of love is that? Just consider the countless women who love you. They followed you everywhere throughout your ministry catering to your material needs. They will follow you on the 'via dolorosa', the sorrowful path to the cross. But they will never want you to die. Go away now, Jesus. go to a country where MOTHER is GOD. That Mother God will never want you to die. She will help you to achieve the fullness of life:life in all its abundance. She will never ever want you to detruncate your youthful life by willing your death.

Go now Jesus, find her because she exists. I, only I will then know where you are and who you are. If you wish, I will even see to it that a scapegoat is nailed to the cross while you make good your escape. Do you remember what the Lord said to Moses? *Make a fiery serpent, and set it on a standard; and it shall come about, that everyone who is bitten, when he looks at it, he will live.* I am the fiery serpent. Look upon me, listen to me…and you will live.

The words the devil uttered had a profound impact on him. He knew what excruciating suffering it would be to be nailed to a cross. Suddenly the dreaded event seemed to come alive. He felt his body being laid on wooden beam while his arms were stretched on either side. He felt the nails being pressed against his wrists. Now the blows of a hammer were falling on the nail heads, piercing his wrists and fastening them to the cross bars. The same was being done to his feet. Every single nerve of his body was wracked with unbearable pain. Now the cross was lifted up and literally allowed to drop into a deep hole, an action that made his body jolt and shudder violently causing excruciating pain while the nails retained it in place.

Then after what seemed an eternity he heard voices addressing him from either side of the cross. He instinctively turned his head to right and left. What he saw was bewildering. Was it real or was it an illusion created by a state of delirium? All the more astonishing was the fact that the two forms also hanging on crosses seemed to be duplicates of himself. The one of the left was telling him: *you saved others but you cannot save yourself. You are a trickster and a fraud. If you are the son of God come down from the cross and bring me down too.* Now he looked to the right. The crucified man on the right had another discourse. He was saying: *we are suffering for our crimes while you are innocent.* Suddenly the reality struck him like a thunderbolt.

Satan, he cried out. Have you followed me even to the cross?

Jesus, the voices were now saying in unison, *your death will be in vain. Your death will never have a decisive effect on humanity. For the ones you will be a trickster and a fraud while for others you will be an innocent man. They will fight with each other to impose their beliefs while the truth, your truth, will die with you. Your partisans will have you resurrected. What they will build on your empty tomb will be their kingdom, their power and their glory. So decide whether you must really die. I can still help you to live.*

NO, no, he screamed into the night. My father and I are ONE. So is our will: it is ONE. It is my will that I die for my fellow human beings to open to them the portals of immortality. My death is not the consequence of an unflinching iron will in my regard. It is an act of LOVE, for greater love has no man that he who lays down his life for his friend.

Then he felt a gentle hand on his shoulder and a known voice telling him: *Jesus, I heard you groaning and agonizing in your sleep.See how you are bathed in sweat Remain calm, Jesus. Be at peace with yourself, It was surely a nightmare, only a nightmare and nothing else but a nightmare.*

CHAPTER 21 - LESSON OF THE PYRAMIDS

✖✖   ✖✖

Soon the foster mother and Miriam became conscious of the irresistible attraction the desert exerted on Jesus. He was acting as if he was drawn by a strange power within him, a power he was not able to resist. What the desert offered him was a sense of the infinite. Such was the effect the vast expanses of sand produced in him. Often when seated in the desert, he felt like a burning bush assailed by inner voices that were leaping upwards like flames all around him. They were deep and probing. His form and identity fused and merged with that of the primordial man presented to him many intriguing features in the creation narrative. The most intriguing of all was the story of the Tree of Life.

As his thoughts tried to unravel that mystery his mind was set alight by the man made mountains the pyramids. They taught him of the yearning and the quest for immortality inscribed in the heart and the mind of man. He learned from the pyramids that the only reality in life was the desire of immortality. It meant that the only real life was the one after death. But it was not as simple as the naïve imagination made it to be.

The proof that the search was unsure and uncertain was in the pyramids. The yearning of man was to return to the same body, the body it has known and lived in. It was the body of the present. Yet that was the case of every reincarnated body. However, each of such bodies had no past. They were each and every one of them bodies that experienced existence as being here and now.

Yet to be doubly sure that the body concerned, the newest and latest of the series, supposedly the most evolved version would be the one that would await the return of the soul, the Pharaohs had their bodies mummified in a manner that not one cell would be displaced from the remains. The loss of even one cell would mean a loss of bodily identity. It would send the soul on an endless search for all eternity, turning after life into a Hades filled with shadows that had lost contact with their physical forms.

Even more compelling than the authenticity of the personal body was the call of that other body that was one flesh and one blood with the departed one. There was the deep belief that when he woke up from his sleep of death, she would be there waiting for him whatever had been the lapse of time in between death and the reawakening. He entertained an unyielding belief that she would recognize him, whatever be his physical aspect through some detail that lay hidden in the recesses of her memory. In the garden that contained the tombs that detail was his voice. It was when he called out her name that recognition had dawned.

As the primordial man and woman, they would be like two fields of gravity the one pulling the other into its zone of magnetic attraction. By his act of solidarity with his consort in the garden he had deceived their common foe and successfully countered his nefarious intent. He had emerged victorious, but at a price, a very heavy one at that, the price of death and separation from her with whom he was one flesh and spirit from age to age and for all ages without end.

In this regard, as in many others, it was once again a myth that stated the truth which evaded history. He saw himself in the mold of a warrior returning home to his consort after a victorious military expedition. He had become one with the hero of the Odyssey. He had conquered by beguiling his foe through an ingenious ruse, that of seemingly succumbing to the temptation of the apple. Yet every desire of an early return was being thwarted by unexpected difficulties. He was being thwarted by angry seas, by monstrous animals and beings in human forms descending from the heavens or surging out of the ocean depths.

There were also among them human giants, superhuman evil forces, born of physical intercourse between debased god-men called fallen angels and the daughters of men. He had confronted mightiest of the earth to obtain the freedom of his followers, putting into practice magic and every occult ritual to obtain their release from the prevailing powers. He had confronted the oceans and their destructive might, ridden the crest of their monumental waves and cleaved them in half, and scaled the mightiest of mountains to be in communion with the heavenly guide.

He had furthermore made every super human effort to act as intermediary between the divine and the human. He had preached a doctrine that stupefied his contemporaries. He had braved the rulers of his time. He had finally delivered himself to the most excruciating and agonizing of deaths in submission to the will of a being he proclaimed to be in an over and beyond called heaven.

And then he rose up from the dead, as he had once risen from a deep slumber, stirred into awakening by the presence of the woman with whom he was one flesh and one spirit. They were the two convergent forms of one circle and the ascending lines of the triangular pyramidal mountain within it, at the supreme point of which they merged into the one divine consciousness and awareness. There the search would end. The unity finally achieved would be infinite, eternal and everlasting.

You think of immortality as an object in the palm of your hand. Look at the pyramids. Consider their unfathomable complexity. The Pharaohs were no ordinary men. They lived in the presence of their gods, hearkening to their voices, offering them ritualistic obeisance, and canvassing their help to merge with them in the after life, the life of immortality. But see their deeds. See the vehicles they built on the sands of time to achieve that end. They are engulfed in mystery and fear of the unknown, a fear totally incompatible with the life they lived in profound communion with the immortal gods considered their predecessors on the throne of Egypt.

CHAPTER 22 - YEARNING FOR IMMORTALITY

This consideration left him silent and thoughtful. What the voice told him was true, entirely true. His thoughts went back to the Pharaohs and to their pyramids. The Pharaohs spent their entire earthly life as a preparation for immortality. Their principal objective in life was personal and individual: it was their own life after death. Immortality was then the cornerstone of their life's endeavour. They would not leave any stone literally unturned to achieve that end.

And so they moved every stone of the desert into place in erecting edifices that defied human ingenuity and imagination, which were meant to last forever as symbols of the triumph of the soul. Their bases led downwards simulating the netherworld, into intricate labyrinthine vaults studded with inconceivable riches and adorned with magical writings, that served as unerring maps for the soul on its onward journey. They laid out an intricate network of paths to mislead pursuers intent on stopping their advance, and especially of tampering with their earthly remains. But most of all these ingenuous creations had to be completely watertight.

The massive stones had to be totally seamless, sealing off every possible outlet through which the soul could be led out by adverse powers, which would totally disorient it and leave it stranded in a no man's space. The field of the soul had necessarily to be the entire dimension of the pyramid's spaces and vaults identified as the universe. Their locations too had been measured with reference to the celestial bodies, the sun, the stars and the planets, with the minutest precision. It was only then the total protection was assured. Only then would the pyramid serve its purpose as the gateway to immortality.

The key to immortality was their earthly remains. They had to be made intact and incorruptible. Not an iota of the body the soul had last known should change. Hence that body was anointed with oils made sacred through magical incantations pleasing to the gods, and was wrapped in layers and layers of impermeable cloth studded and embellished with talismans, amulets, and every conceivable magical device. The body was laid in the sarcophagus to await the return of the wandering soul. The riches the Pharaoh had accumulated during his reign were all placed at the disposal of the wandering soul so that it would not suffer from any want material or spiritual during its journey to immortality.

The walls of those underground passages would be covered with secret codes only the wandering soul could read and interpret. No error was permissible and no error was humanly possible. Such was the care the priests and scribes would take in that regard. When the soul returned as the all conquering warrior and identified his body, then the body and soul reunited would rise again and take their place among the immortals and live forever in power and glory in a kingdom without end. His victory would be the victory of all. His victory that transformed him into the invincible sun would guarantee light and life to all.

The civilization of the Pharaohs was one that laid its trust in myths that were more in the ambit of imagination than of reason. Imagination was not bound to a time and space sequence. In imagination the sense of time was annulled as was also the sense of space. For such civilizations the Eternal was not bound by time and space. For the Eternal there was no 'from now to then' or from 'here to there'. The Eternal experienced everything as a total all encompassing uninterrupted vision in an immobile unmoving NOW. And so he learned to distinguish between reality and truth. That awareness changed his attitude towards life. Now all that mattered to him was the truth and nothing else.

His preoccupation with the pyramids and their significance led him to the awareness that the most vital force in human life is Imagination. Imagination is the silent creative force of man. It uses impressions left by time in his senses, his mind, and memory, as its raw material. Time is the waters over which imagination hovers. Such time, the raw material of the imagination, is an ocean which the imagination transforms into an ocean of story. Memory the glimmering waters offers its ever fluctuating forms to the creative force of the imagination. Then the imagination strengthens what is vague giving it a recognizable form and identity. Memory and imagination are the buoys on which floundering senses and reason support themselves for survival.

The words of the scriptures flashed like lightening before his inner eye: *your old men shall see dreams and your young men shall see visions*. Both visions and dreams are within the sphere of the imaginary and are outside the pale of reason. The truths he knew and inculcated by his sacred scriptures were the eruption of the eternal through the medium of visions and dreams. For a man named Paul, the truth of his existence was founded purely on a vision. Never had he met, seen, or heard the man he deified worldwide. Furthermore he had hardly associated with those who had. The mission of Paul was a one man show. For his parents Mary and Joseph, their existence was founded on dreams. Visions and dreams the playground of which was imagination were accepted as being the surest medium of communication between human beings and the divine.

CHAPTER 23 - SATAN AND SALVATION

✖ ✖   ✖ ✖

He was drawn out of his ever persistent reveries by a voice. *Come, he heard the voice calling out to him, come with me deeper into the desert.* Then he felt himself being wafted through the air and placed on the summit of a mountain. There the voice returned.

The stones were the medium of immortality for the Pharaohs. Turn these stones into bread and make them the bread of life by consuming them.

He touched the stones tendered to him and to his surprise they were transformed into loaves of bread.

Now eat said the voice. He obeyed and ate. He felt a great transformation occurring within him. He felt his body being transformed into a giant pyramid that spanned the earth and the heavens. The immense silence in which he was engulfed was only broken by the voice which continued to speak.

From stone to bread, from bread to body, and from body to way, truth and life, it said. *Your body is now bread. Do with it what you please. Your body is now the medium and the guarantee of immortality. The stones were the medium of immortality for the Pharaohs. It was their way to the truth and to life. As for you and your followers, it is your body: your body, the way, the truth and the life.* So saying the voice left him.

I am the way, the truth and the life... I am the way, the truth and the life, the sound was echoed back through the vault of the heavens. It was as if heaven had endorsed him and established him as the one and only way that was also the truth and the life.

As the scene changed, he was in a simple room surrounded by disciples. They had assembled for supper, but it was a supper with a difference. Everyone felt that something unexpected was going to happen. They felt a strange foreboding as regards their leader who sat at the head of the table. He held a loaf of bread in his hands and he was offering it to them as food. Yet his words made a difference. They were just as unexpected as they were bewildering. He was calling the bread his body.

He then remembered the words that had gushed out from his mouth: *I am the living bread that came down from heaven. If anyone eats of this bread, he will live forever. And the bread that I will give for the life of the world is my flesh. Eat of this,* he was telling them, *for this is my body.* From the medium of immortality the stones of the pyramids had become the bread of eternal life for the souls emerging from darkness into light.

One bread, one flesh, one life for one and all. A body destined to die and be returned to dust had been transformed into an object of glory: *the glory which You have given Me I have given to them, that they may be one, just as We are one.* It was within this divine pyramid, the human body, that lay the kingdom, the glory and the power of the ONE God. By transforming his body into bread, the one had paved the way for the many to become one, sharing in one and the same divine glory.

He had attained a new understanding of himself. The new pyramid, the edifice that was the medium of immortality for all who entered within it was his body. He who ate of the bread that was his body would not hunger and will live forever. His body being the pathway to and guarantee of immortality, no one who became one with that body would need to store worldly riches for his eternal conservation and well being. Knowing the lot of the pyramids at the hands of thieves, robbers and treasure hunters he would admonish his followers with the words: *"Do not store up for yourselves treasures on earth, where moth and rust destroy, and where thieves break in and steal. But store up for yourselves treasures in heaven, where neither moth nor rust destroys, and where thieves do not break in or steal."*

Jesus, he heard a soft whispering by his side and the touch of a gentle hand on his shoulders. You were speaking in your sleep. Is everything alright?

Yes, he replied calmly. Miriam I had a dream, or was it a dream. It was so real, as real as what I see around me now.

I know, she said, because I was there.

Where? he answered, trying to recollect the scene he had just experienced with a view to identifying her presence.

Jesus, the beloved disciple, the one with the head on your breast was me. Jesus, you not only experience dreams, you make them to be. The spirit that hovered over the waters of time and made the earth and the heavens to be, that is you. You infuse the void and the empty with light, that light which is the life of men. The mirages that arise in your mind are oases for mankind. Did not the psalms speak of one who makes us lie down in green pastures and leads us beside quiet waters? You are the *light of the world*; he who follows you shall not walk in the darkness, but shall have the Light of life.

The revelation of the pyramids put him in the grip of a new enthusiasm. His wanderings in the desert increased. He learned that both the path to plenitude as well as the path to solitude and loneliness was the same. It was the way to fullness and it was the way to emptiness. Fullness and emptiness were two sides of the same apparent reality. He learned that solitude and loneliness is the land of the strong. Indeed, when the going became daring, it was the daring that got going.

Jesus realized that there were great similarities between the desert and the ocean. There surfaces were never still. Countless waves arose at the behest of every passing wind. The bigger dunes appeared like big waves. Their surfaces were also ever undulating. From both arose unexpected storms. As in water so too in the desert sands, the surface would yield under his feet and make him sink. When he walked on the undulating desert sands, he often had the distinct impression that he was walking on the sea.

It was on one such occasion that he saw a scene from the future that engrossed his mind to such an extent that it was for all purposes happening before his eyes. At his behest his disciples were putting out to sea. They were all hungry and needed a catch of fish for their supper. While they were away, he lay on the desert sands and fell asleep. What he saw next seemed to shake him awake. His mind was conjuring up a nightmare. He saw the boat of his disciples in grave danger. A terrible storm was shaking the sea of Galilee and the boat was being buffeted like a leaf in the winds. He saw hands outstretched towards him and frantic pleas for urgent immediate succour.

Then his spirit rose and led out his form still in deep sleep, making it to wade over the waters to where the boat was courting disaster. He stretched his hands towards the surging waves and told them: be still. The storm was gone and calm had returned to the sea. He heard his disciples say: *who is this whom even the winds and sea obey*. When he woke up what he felt was the moving surface of the desert beneath him, like the writhing coils of a giant serpent. Was it the desert, the serpent or the sea that had made the reality of his vision to materialize? Really it did not matter in the least as these three factors had played preponderant roles in his life both in his years of formation as well as during those of his maturity. They were as dice that determined his destiny from the very inception in the garden of Eden, through the crossing of the red sea, and his encounters with the diabolic and the divine.

CHAPTER 24 - CONTEXT OF THE GODS

In the desert what attracted him most were the high places which he sought out and climbed to their very summits. From there he watched the rising sun. In the night he experienced the desert cold and saw the moon take its position in the sky. He watched the countless stars that blinked at him like celestial eyes. He saw the vultures that prey on animals, and the skulls of cattle strewn on the ground around him. He saw serpents appearing from and disappearing under rocky outgrowths. All around him were rocks of all shapes and hues. Often he even slept on the mountain summits assisting time again at the ever unfailing sunrise. He realized how that light was the life of men. He realized how it was the dream of the Pharaohs to merge with the sun and ensure light and life to their land and to the world. He understood why the sun god was the primeval God of every pantheon.

His wanderings sometimes brought him to the limits of total exhaustion. He felt extremely hungry and thirsty. Under such conditions he began seeing visions and his imagination placed him in strange situations. He beat on the rocks with sticks thinking he was Moses, and he bit into little stones imagining them to be pieces of manna fallen from the sky. When he slept, he imagined himself in the personality of Elijah and saw angels coming towards him with warm oven baked bread and jugs of water.

In the throes of delirium he imagined himself a god of the Egyptian pantheon, placed in an Egyptian temple clothed with the sun, the moon and stars with faces and head gear like the forms of the desert animals, with leonine faces, horns, sharp aquiline beaks and winged arms. He imagined himself as the god of the dead and of life, a status he saw himself conferred with after his own death and resurrection. He saw himself crossing the mythical waters to assume his over lordship of the kingdom of the dead, and finding his way with ease through subterranean corridors through which the souls of the dead must pass.

And then the climax came. He felt himself as being on the summit of a mountain. What happened then was breathtaking. The sun was expanding and filling the heavenly vault, which became one mass of light. Then it opened, revealing a dazzling interior that impeded all visibility. And out of it riding on clouds was the figure of a man, a real son of man, who was descending towards him. He was overwhelmed with an incredible feeling of happiness and joy. The figure continued its descent, neared the summit on which he stood, and positioned itself exactly on the place on the summit he was occupying.

It was then that he realized that his form had merged with that of the son of man. Such was the transfiguration he had undergone. He realized that he had merged with the sun, even more, that it was he the sun. Yes, it was he, the sun. His mind was flooded with the light that was life He was heralding the triumph of life over death, of life over darkness. He was the way, the truth and the life. Heaven and earth was filled with his glory and rent the air with cries of hosannah God Most High.

And now the earth was quivering and trembling like the womb of a woman in labour. The ocean within it was like the water bag out of which a new born was about to emerge. The womb was expanding and reaching up to the summit on which the son of man stood gazing at the evolving scene. Soon the earth had reached the dizzy heights of the mountain summit, become the footstool of the invincible sun, the son of man, and delivery was taking place. What came out of the womb earth was a woman. The earth had eclipsed the sun. Scenes were changing and transformations were taking place as in the blinking of one eyelid. When the bewildering process ended what stood on the summit was the woman with the sun, the invincible sun, lying in her arms and become her son. The woman was telling him: *you are my beloved son, this day have I begotten thee*. What seemed to be angelic voices were acclaiming her: *Thou art the queen of the earth and of the heavens*.

As the vision faded he sat transfixed by what he had witnessed and experienced. The words the woman spoke to him were having an almost deafening impact on him. She was saying: *you are my beloved son, this day have I begotten thee*. He felt himself being transfigured and standing on the summit of Mount Sinai closeted with the divine law giver.

He heard the laws smitten into the stone slabs. One read: *thou shall not place other gods in my place*. And now a strong wind was lifting him bodily from that summit and bringing him down to where his people were worshiping a golden calf. He was now changing his forms as the spirit willed. He was experiencing events that human reason could never conceive. He the invincible sun was lying in the arms of the mother goddess.

Mother and son

As he turned his face towards her and uttered the word, mother, her face was undergoing a metamorphosis. What was happening was taking an infinity of time or so it seemed. When finally the transfiguration was complete the face was that of a cow surmounted with semicircular horns that contained the sun. His mother, the mother goddess was holding him, the invincible sun in the form of a calf turned into gold by the divine rays of the heavenly object, aloft on her head, and displaying him to the heavens shouting her joy with the words: *this is my beloved son, this day have I begotten him.*

The next moment he was looking on aghast and in convulsive anguish as the people, the chosen people of God were taking up iron rods and striking the figure of the cow and its first born calf, reducing it to smithereens. *No, no, he screamed, no, do not do that to us, to the Goddess of the heavens and the earth, and to me, her only son.* And then the vision was over. He was raising his arms towards the heavens while tears of excruciating suffering and anguish were pouring down his face. He wept and wept bitter drops of tears that turned into blood as they were absorbed by the earth under his feet.

As he yearned for the ever evasive sleep, the scenes he abhorred were still unfolding before him. He saw the golden calf being beaten to death by a people calling themselves the people of God. He saw the goddess images of the woman depicted as the bandit queen of the bible, Jezebel, subject to wanton destruction, and their priests slaughtered by the imagined order of God.

The enigma that is woman

The fate meted out to goddess images was also that meted out to her living forms. The images that propped up within him mind were so overwhelming, that they continued even when sheer fatigue was bringing him to the brink of sleep. He saw a woman who, without the least shred of biblical evidence, was denuded and paraded before the eyes of a people, called the chosen people of the New Covenant, as a harlot, possessed of seven devils, meaning the seven deadly sins. He saw her eternally on her knees before the bastion of a male priesthood calling themselves the representatives of God on earth, pleading for forgiveness with entreaties that she be spared the ritualistic death by stoning.

By her side was another woman, who had brought forth what, in the eyes of the law was a fatherless child, whom the law, the God given law, pronounced as meriting death by stoning, being exalted and made to ascend bodily to heaven, adorned with all the most glorious titles mankind could give to her, and literally merged with the infinite, eternal and everlasting Godhead. *Miriam*, he screamed when recognition dawned. *How can this be? How can you be virgin and whore?* How can you be derided, scorned and heaped with opprobrium, and exalted to the heavens at the same time? It seemed to him that the body of the woman had become a source of embarrassment to an all male hierarchy clothed in costumes of mythological origin, assuming rule over space and time, and sitting on thrones that are the hearts of men.

His questions made him probe deeper into the subject. The body of the woman was placing these individuals in a state of mental and physical disequilibrium. On the one hand they were exalting a woman stripped of her inborn and inherent capacity and right to experience physical pleasure, and proposing her as example and model of womanhood. On the other hand they were trampling on a woman who asserted the rights she possessed over her own body, demonizing her, and making her out to be a manifestation of the most loathful seven vices.

Why this duplicity as regards woman? He asked

The reply took no time to come. I will tell you, the voice within him said. This dual vision of woman is nothing but a strategy of self glorification, of self divinization. Stripping one woman's body of her capacity for pleasure and making her inaccessible to them, they deem necessary to renounce lusting after her. By trampling on another woman's body which is accessible to them, offering them all the pleasures they seek, they pretend to achieve the same purpose. What they put on display in both cases is the resultant make-believe purity of their own bodies, which is the very ground of their claim to rule over space and time, and to make the hearts of men their throne.

An agonizing question remained on his lips, even as he surrendered himself to the arms of sleep. Is there a place in this world where the female nature would be extolled irrespective of the form it donned, and irrespective of considerations of virginity or whoredom attributed to her?

CHAPTER 25 - NEW EARTH: NEW CREATION

Now his interior vision was changing. The sleepless eye of his subconscious mind was looking into the prism of time. What he saw and experienced within it provided him with the consolation the Torah had robbed him of. He saw himself being transfigured, stripped of his time stitched mantle of Jewishness, and clothed in the loin cloth of a distant civilization. He found himself immersed in a crowd that feted an animal as the mother goddess. The cow and her offspring were being paraded through the streets by the tumultuous multitude. The animal forms were decked in gilded and dazzling embellishments. They were being offered the choicest of foods. They were being accorded the honours due to their divinity in a ceremony which was an age old cult and ritual.

It was a liturgy that celebrated womanhood in the form of an animal, an animal that was the giver of life, love and nourishment to all humanity: a form that represented woman as mother, lover and life long companion. Borne on the wave of an unbridled enthusiasm he was crying to the four winds addressing his joy to the divinized animal form with the heartfelt words: *thy people shall be my people, and thy God my God.*

That brief interlude that had revealed mother earth in her bovine form had come and gone. As the scene faded he found himself once again on the summit of the mountain as before. The woman of his vision and he stood a while facing each other, and the time that passed seemed an eternity. Sensing that the scene was now beginning to fade, he clutched at the figure that was holding him to her breast and shouted the panic stricken word that gushed from his mouth: *mother*. What he retained most of this vision was that of the son of man descending on a cloud into the arms of his mother the earth. So mesmerized was his mind and so imbued with this experience, he would at every available occasion refer to himself as '*the son of man coming seated on the clouds*'.

As he called himself the son of man coming on the clouds and descending to earth, his mind was vivid with memories of himself in other human forms that also descended to earth on the clouds. He saw himself in the form of another man named Enoch who, just as he, was pleasing to God. Indeed it was a man who had not seen death. He was so pleasing to God that God took him to himself. God took him to himself because the earth, pure mother earth, had been sullied with impurities of the worst kind. The just man, the earthly form of the beloved son pleasing to him, he had taken up to the heavens. So too it was with God's son in another human form who had taken the name of Elijah. Him too God had taken up to heaven. Their bodies had not seen decay and corruption.

His mind now went back to the temple where his foster mother was a priestess, where his sister Miriam was also officiating in the same role. He too was in the bloodline of priests, of the order of Melchisedech, a priest without earthly father and earthly mother, a priest that appeared out of time and space, the earthly realization of the dream world that is eternity. Yet another whom God had taken to his bosom, and spared the passage through death. Whatever be the human form the spirit of God endowed his son with, God would see that that form would not see corruption.

The spirit blows where it will. One knows not whence it comes and whence it goes. Under the action of the spirit the mind and the body were as prime matter. He remembered telling those who opposed him that God could raise children to Abraham from the stones that littered his paths. So too can God raise his son when and where he will from any primordial matter, for all matter is fundamentally primordial before his will and in his hands.

* * * * *

From these entire episodes one thing was clear. It was that God's will would only be done in heaven. The task of mother earth would be to engender human forms that would be pleasing to God and whom God would take up to heaven. The victory of evil would only be a sorrowful facade, a staged drama for the credulous. It would be a Trojan horse, an apparent surrender for the delight of the forces of evil, just as had been the apparent surrender of the primordial couple to the viles of the devil in the Garden of Eden.. Evil would revel in the illusion of reality: the passing reality that was a scene enacted on the stage of time with transient forms and identities that made their entry and exit as demanded by the staged scene.

He saw looking once again at the statue of the mother and son, the mother goddess and her god-son. Now the picture in his mind was clear. What that statue represented was a new earth and a new heaven, a new creation. It was a creation the cornerstones of which were the virgin earth in the form of the virgin mother goddess, the queen of the heaven and earth, and of her son descended from the beyond, from across the great divide, riding on the clouds.

This new creation would be the prototype of all creation myths elaborated by all nations and all peoples, of every race, hue and religion with which to find consolation as regards their human condition. The ideal of a pure mother and a pure son and a heavenly existence where the will of God would prevail was the dream of mankind. It was a heavenly order that was being ushered before his eyes, a heavenly order of death and resurrection, and it was that heavenly order of which he was the way, the truth and the life.

CHAPTER 26 - VANQUISHING DEATH

Deeply merged with the spirit and possessed by it, he saw himself walking along a path surrounded by throngs of passers by. Then he heard the sound of an approaching funeral procession. As the procession approached the place where he was, the people regrouped themselves on either side to free the passage for the bier. It was being carried shoulder high by four stout men. After them came the mother of the deceased totally distraught, weeping and wailing at her loss. Her hands were stretched out towards the heavens and she was calling God to witness her sorrow. The dead person was her only son. The bier had by now reached the place where he stood. He was feeling the promptings of the spirit urging him to act. He instinctively put up his hand in an imperious gesture beckoning the bearers to stop.

They looked at him with amazement tinged with curiosity. Sensing that this was someone with superhuman powers the mother came towards him suppliantly, loudly lamenting what had befallen her son. 'My only son, Lord, she wailed, *my only son. He was the support, the only support of my failing years'* she cried out loud and heartrendingly. So saying, she embraced him in sheer desperation. What he felt was the surging of a whirlpool of compassion out of the depthless ocean of love.

His memory was now displaying on the screen of his mind an event buried in the sands of time. He saw himself clothed in the form of Elijah confronted by a widow whose son had died. The boy had died. He was dead. No one had ever been raised from the dead before--at least, not in the record of Scripture up to this point. It was the same history repeating itself in what for him was the ever present NOW. He was now stretching himself over the child three times and then turning to the mother with the triumphant words: *See your son is alive!*

With this his mind was stretching itself over the future. He was seeing a widow, her arms outstretched to the heavens asking God to give her back her son, her only son who himself lay outstretched and dead on a cross. *Lord, my only son,* she was crying out in her agony, *my only son. He was the support, the only support of my failing years*

Tears were streaming down his face as he faced the widow. His memory was reverberating with the sound of the words: *Lord, my only son, my only son. He was the support, the only support of my failing years*. With one arm around her he approached the bier and removed the covering cloth from the corpse. With her dead son exposed to her view once again the mother fell on the ground in a swoon while relatives supported her. All eyes were now on him.

When he came out of his trance, he appeared totally exhausted. He saw himself surrounded by his apostles.

They had been perturbed by the time that he had been away and had come to seek him. What they saw made them breathless. The still figure of the Master, his eyes closed with traces of tears on them totally oblivious of himself and everything around him. Now they sat in awe around him hardly daring to break the silence that pervaded the extraordinary scene. It took him some time to re-find his bearings. Then he gradually opened his eyes and saw them. Yet no one spoke.

Where have you been master, one of them finally dared to ask.

The spirit of my father took me away, he said. *I just restored a dead son to his mother*, he said again.

He told them what he had experienced of the funeral cortege, and his divine intervention that gave life to a dead youth. His description was so vivid and detailed that they could picture it occurring before their eyes. It was as if it was happening then and there. The spaces of their minds had undergone a miraculous change. They literally saw, and heard and experienced what was being narrated. Their minds were enraptured with wonderment and their hearts were throbbing hard. What they felt and sensed and experienced in their bodies and in their minds, was of a happening that had taken place before their eyes. It had happened somewhere, but did that matter? What mattered was that God had resurrected a human being from the dead.

The disciples still watched him in utter amazement. His eyes were looking far beyond the horizons and what they were fixed on was a man hanging on a cross, his heart perforated by a spear, brought down and laid in a tomb. Him God had raised from the dead. In that resurrection an immense multitude that filled the earth would rejoice and exult. Yet they had not seen it happening. Such was the feeling that prevailed among the disciples. They could only say: *Indeed, you are the son of God.*

As for him, he had issued from a dream, he had lived this dream and he would walk in his dream back to where he came from, a kingdom that was a dream, leaving behind his dream for others to conceive, follow and realize. The stunned multitude turned to each other in disbelief. *Who is this man?* they asked. *Who else can raise up the dead, but God.*

CHAPTER 27 - THE QUESTION OF GOD

Who else can raise up the dead, but God. The phrase did not leave his mind, but absorbed it and demanded a deeper probe. As if in answer to the query regarding the mystery of God, he saw himself standing in an open forum in Athens. Here religious orators extolled the virtues and attributes of their gods, the gods, local and imported, of the Greek pantheon. They were not all gods that had emerged out of the depths of Greek religious consciousness. They were gods begotten in the minds and hearts of humanity. What was their origin? Egyptian, Babylonian? Sumerian? Persian? Greek, Indian?

Who cared about the whence or the where from? It did not finally matter. They had ushered themselves on the world scene, the stage of dreams, out of the yearnings of the human heart and mind. The names by which they were designated or the epithets of history or myth employed in their regard did not matter in the least. What mattered was the truth, the truth that without them mankind would be embarking on stormy seas without stars to guide them or be like rudderless sails-less aimlessly drifting rafts. They were stars that helped human beings to navigate from the shores of their illusory little 'selfs' to the truth and reality: the GREAT SELF that they all were.

As he wandered around the forum he saw countless images that assumed the forms the gods had donned to reveal themselves to their adepts. It was then that his eyes alighted on a faceless bi-sexual statue standing on a stone foundation. On it was an inscription which read: *to the unknown God*. Its significance struck him immediately. This was the ideal platform for him to launch into the deep. The faceless sculpture was an invitation to inspired orators to don the mask of the god of their choice. Yet no mask or form could represent the God he was about to announce. He stood on a makeshift podium set up by its side and shouted to the four winds. *This is the God that I proclaim, the unknown, hidden, unfathomable, faceless Godhead inaccessible to the human mind.*

He was now recalling his encounter at a well with a woman who was not of his race and creed. He had promised her living waters which would quench her thirst forever. Her fathers, she had said, searched for the springs of the eternal, the infinite and the unending in sanctuaries situated on mountains and other places just as did the crowd that he was now confronting. But such gods, the ones conceived in human minds and formed by human hands could not satiate their thirst.

He was now hearing the words the woman was addressing to him. *Sir*, she said, *give me this water so that I won't get thirsty and have to keep coming here to draw water.*

What was now reverberating in his mind were the delirious cries of a crowd as they made their way to a source of water, a river. They were shouting: RAMA NAMA SATYA HE – Only God is true: only God is truth; the only truth there is is God. Draw from the source that is God. That source is within you. Only that water will quench the thirst of humanity for ever.

This truth he proclaimed to her when he told her: *the time has come when the true God will no more be worshiped in temples, in sanctuaries, on mountains or other places of worship. He is spirit and he is truth.*

In the batting of an eyelid his location had changed. He felt he was different, different in skin colour, in form, in culture and language. He was in a far away place, in a place of mystics, of god-men, in a place called the land of the gods. Below the path that led to his make shift abode a river flowed, a river that had its origin in snow clad mountain peaks and which was venerated during countless ages to present times. It was a river that served as a mother goddess, the womb and the tomb to its adepts. On its banks were held perennial rites and ceremonies in expression of the belief that she was an eternal life giving force. On it were placed the statues of the mightiest gods of the pantheon. They seemed to emerge from the womb of this mother goddess and seemingly remained attached voluntarily to the umblical cords that bound them to her. It was a public averment that without her they were nothing, that they derived all their power from her. She was SHAKTHI. Only she could give birth to the divine nature within them.

He spent his time walking along its banks or seated facing it in contemplation of its divinity. And as the life giving forces emerged within him, he felt his physical form becoming an empty shell, while he was filled with a fullness and plenitude that removed him from the stage of time, clothing him with a power that created and sustained the universe. He did not know how long such trances lasted, but that they were long indeed very long was obvious judging from the length and proportion of his beard and the extent to which his flesh had crumpled.

There was something remarkable about such episodes. Every time he came back to the consciousness of physical nature, he found himself surrounded by continuous gatherings around him adopting postures of veneration and homage. He felt the garlands that had been placed around his neck while the spaces around him were filled with flowers and food. They knew that he was in the throes of an experience which no eye has seen, no ear has heard and which no human heart had conceived. They could only be before him in awe, in reverence and in homage, and show their esteem with all the means at their disposal.

The vision had passed away. He had regained his posture and was once again aware of what was transpiring before him. It was then that his finger moved from the one to the other among his audience, pinpointing each and everyone. The words he uttered bewitched and mystified them. They had the effect of a thunderbolt from the blues. He said: Thou art THAT - *infinite Being-Awareness-Bliss*. God is not an object to be touched, to be seen and heard. He is to be experienced. And when that happens, it is once and for all. It may not happen in one lifetime or even in many. It could come after eons of existences. Do not be frightened by the passage of time because wherever and whenever you live you will only experience time as HERE and NOW. You will neither live in a past nor in a future, you can be nowhere else but here and now in an unfailing present.

What gripped his mind as he uttered these words was the image of a vagabond preacher who preached a parable to a great multitude of followers. The parable of the labourers and the Lord's vineyard. They had gone for work at different times of the day, some in the early hours of the morning while other reached there late in the afternoon. Yet the salary given to each was the same, the duration of work being of no consequence. So too would it be as regards the realization of one's true Self. For some it would take eons, for others, ages, and for yet others, just a watch in the night. When that happens, it would be in a permanent enduring NOW without end. Time would have been transcended. Its illusory nature would have been unveiled.

Nothing will change your destiny, he was telling his listeners, which is to be still, outside the flow of time, merge with infinite, eternal and immortal awareness and consciousness, and know that you are THAT, the mystery that is God. Only he will know who undergoes that experience, for that experience is not communicable. That is the reason why such human beings leave everyone and everything and go... go wherever the spirit leads them, into deserts, to mountains, to solitary landscapes of snow clad regions, to the sources of holy rivers, to be alone. Their solitude and loneliness was a foretaste of immortality, a foretaste of being unique in the fullness and the plenitude that is the consciousness of God.

CHAPTER 28 - QUESTIONS REQUIRING ANSWERS

His mind was now opening up new vistas and changing scenes. It was as if eons were succeeding each other before the unblinking eyes of the eternal presence. He saw himself making the same declarations in other places, before other crowds. They were now rushing towards him to lay hold of him and drag him to a mountain top, to hurl him over the precipice into abysmal depths below. The he saw similar crowds taking stones to hurl at him. He saw himself having donned the physical form of others bound to the stake over and over again by those who professed to follow him, and burned alive. He heard unbelievable declarations made to justify the massacre of entire populations. He heard the delegate of one who pretended to be his successor say, when asked how a believer could be distinguished from a heretic: *kill them all, let God sort them out*, the delegate had said.

He saw his teachings brought into ridicule and made a mockery of by lay rulers for their purposes. He saw books written about his teachings buried in the desert sands to escape destruction by adverse forces. He had heard resounding debates about his person, as to whether he was a historical figure or a myth, recast in the mold of the myths of antiquity. In fact the question has been posed to him by a seeker of the truth as he walked along the banks of the sacred river.

Reverend, there are religions that claim authenticity on the grounds that they are historical while others said to be of mythical character are down graded.

His reply was spontaneous and direct. He said: *neither history nor myth matters, it is the truth they connote*. He knew that the more history recedes into the past, the more it becomes the stuff of imagination just as what myths are.

Lord, a voice broke the ocean of silence within him. *Tell us more about this THAT, the mystery hidden within us.*

That mystery is the divine consciousness that we are called to discover within ourselves and with which to merge. That divine consciousness is the unborn. That unborn itself can never be born and can never die. Deep within you, you are that unborn, and so neither can you be born nor can you die. We are each and every one of us the divine consciousness in a human form. That divine consciousness lies hidden in the labyrinthine depths of the mind and the heart of every human being. We are each and everyone God who has donned the form of our little self and is walking within us towards the discovery of the GREAT SELF that he is.

Lord, another said. My mind is disturbed and perplexed. The scriptures tell us that we are tainted with the sin that our first parents are said to have committed. The scriptures tell us of a God-man, a savior a Messiah to come who will atone for our original sin by undergoing an excruciating death. How can that be?

The question had a deep impact on him. His thoughts centered on himself. Who am I, he asked himself again and again. Am I the literal son of God or a mystery and a metaphor, a voice within, the divine consciousness in a human form? His was a voice in the wilderness, the pillar of fire and the white cloud that led man through the desert of life to the Promised Land: the consciousness that is God.

What is man before the immensity of God, he answered back. What is a drop of water, a speck of dust or a blade of grass or anything else for that matter, in the unending, evolving infinite immensity that is the universe? Could one such ever be an affront to the universe? Could the act of a creature ruffle its creator to such a point that it would draw on the erring ones an implacable death sentence to be inexorably passed down from birth to birth, affecting all humanity until the end of time? Could such an error on the part of a creature necessitate a life sacrificing atonement by God himself, whatever be the name and form he assumed? Could anything that a puny creature did, impose on him a sense of guilt that thrusts the devil and eternal hellfire into his conscience, transforming the image of God into a ruthless tyrant, of one who watches, pursues and punishes, even with the supreme penalty of eternal death?

~~~ ~~~ ~~~

CHAPTER 29 - THE COSMIC FORM

He was now undergoing an inner upheaval. He watched the present change in its layout and reality. He saw a violent crowd came towards him dragging a semi-nude hapless woman. She was being taken to be stoned to death for adultery. Now adultery was a sin that figured in the Ten Commandments given to Moses by God himself. It was by chance that he stood in their way. Seeing the popular and unorthodox preacher they stopped before him to galvanize his support as well for the stoning. When they asked him for his judgment about the crime and the punishment, the answer they received brought them to a standstill. *'He who has not sinned, let him throw the first stone'* he told them.

The crowd had dispersed shamefacedly, and now he was telling the woman: Has no one condemned you?

No one Lord, had been the answer.

So he told her, neither will I condemn you.

A human spirit merged with the divine consciousness had refused to judge, leave alone condemn a woman who had sinned against the official commandment of God, a sin that merited death by stoning.

Memories came flooding into his mind, Episodes of the past were rushing for recognition. He had never played the role of a judge. *Judge not and you shall not be judged* was his leitmotif. Then he heard a voice shouting from the crowd.

Someone in the crowd was telling him, *Teacher, tell my brother to divide the inheritance with me.*

But he said to him, *Man, who made me a judge or arbitrator over you?*

His whole nature rebelled against such a thought. But it inevitably led him into situations of conflict with colossuses with feet of clay, with owners of glass houses who indulged in the pastime of throwing stones at those outside.

At that moment Jesus felt his physical form merging with the spaces within his mind and undergoing a change. He found himself in surroundings that were radically different from those in which he was a moment ago. The path he was treading was intersected by many small rivers. He felt chilly as a cold wind blew through the open spaces. He stepped into rivers at each river's edge. As he looked into the waters he felt his spirit hovering over it. The ripples blurred his vision, but he kept his eyes focused on the undulating surface.

And then he saw himself. His skin had taken a different hue and his head was shaved. The eyes that looked out of the waters had lowered eyelids. Those eyes looked inwards. People around him made room for him to enter the ferry and a seat was offered to him on a wooden bench. He repeated his actions of entering into the ferry and out of it at several locations, and then he made his way to an orchard. People were following him and their attitudes were those of deep respect. All this while a thought was playing on his mind. What was really that apple? He asked himself again. That fruit was the embodiment of earthly desire, of greed and of craving.

What he experienced now was beyond imagination. He was seated under a tree dressed in the garb of an ascetic of a distant land, of a distant clime. The tree was not unknown to him. It was majestic in its proportions with a canopy that rivaled the heavenly vault, It was a virtual forest with trunks descending from its umbrella-shaped roof like the ladders of Jacob. It was a virtual tree of knowledge. Legs crossed, seated upright, his back against the trunk of the tree he was, in the role of a sage, imparting his teachings to avid listeners.

To the wheel of greed and craving we are bound, he said. But what do we crave for: for forms, for forms that are void and empty. Impermanent, alas, are all forms, They arise and fall. Having arisen, they eventually cease. *Everything that rises and ceases is without substance. Everything such thing is a dream, and so is also the dreamer, a dream.*

Lord, have you conquered this human condition: the condition of greed and craving? a voice asked.

After a short pause he answered. All that we are pivots around our self conferred identity. Our identity is the builder of the burning house of our senses. We prefer to burn within it than seek refuge outside it. But I have seen and recognized him, the builder, and addressed to him these words: *O house-builder, you are seen! You will not build this house again. For your rafters are broken and your ridgepole shattered. My mind has reached the Unconditioned; I have attained the destruction of craving.*

What is that Unconditioned, Lord. What is it like, Master? Tell us what it is so that we could shed all craving knowing what we are entering into. Is it like lying weightless on the surface of waters, enjoying the beating of the gentle waves and the soothing breeze? Is it a mindless, bodyless state? It is an experience of the senseless and the void? What is it?

It is That, That which cannot be expressed by substanceless thought. Now *all that we are a grounded on our thoughts, are made up of our thoughts and result from our thoughts.* If such was the nature of that which is the ground, the composition and the result of our existence, then so must it be with our existence itself. But there is an uncreate that neither comes nor goes nor stands; neither dies nor is born. It is without change; it is the eternal which never originates and never passes away. It is That, the end of the suffering which is transience, change and mutation: of appearing and disappearing. It is the Consciousness of the ONE. It is the divine manna which he only knows who receives it. It is the experience of the Sun of Enlightenment, and it is within you.

How can we realize that unconditioned, that uncreate which is the Sun of Enligtenment, which is within us?

Leave your identity, the one your form has clothed itself with to play your role on the stage of life and which is your self. That identity is the builder of that house of darkness, that house in flames, that you are. That identity, your self is the mask of time, of relentless aimlessly drifting time, of unending time, the theater of vanity and nothingness. It is darkness displaying an illusory face of light. Behind that mask is the Real Person that you are. Do not cling to the mask of time, your illusory self, do not grasp it, do not attach yourself to it. Just let go. Let go of greed and craving which are its primary attributes. Thus only will our self-made house collapse and disappear forever. Thus will you abide in your REAL SELF in the unmoving, immovable NOW, experiencing the DIVINE CONSCIOUSNESS which is the light that is life.

CHAPTER 30 – THE MANY 'SELFS'

He was now alone, and leaning against the tree he fell asleep. What he saw next was a densely populated house that was burning. Flames were sprouting everywhere, even leaping up and devouring the roof. All was burning. Yet the people were not moving, preferring to remain within and be consumed by the fire.

Why? he asked as he witnessed the curious phenomenon.

Because we prefer to live with what we know, with what we are accustomed to, with our proven way of life, with our actual forms that need no transformations, than to venture out into what we do not know and become other than what we know we are, was the answer forthcoming from the willing sufferers engulfed in the flames. He lay silent, sunk in the spaces within him as if trying to awaken from a dream.

The words of the willing inmates of the house on flames came back over and over again into his mind. They wished to be the 'self' they knew, whatever be the consequence, be it their own destruction. But was their argument true? He asked himself. Can someone in the throes of incessant change, ever on the move with the wheels of time and space inscribed into the composition of his very existence, ever know who he really is? Was such an individual really one, or was he the many clinging to the illusion of his sameness?

He realized that the endeavour of each and everyone was to merge all the 'selfs' revived by memory and imagination and which one's form had identified itself with, with the self one conceived as doing oneself proud and revealing the best of him. Yet he knew what a futile endeavour that was. The 'self' of the 'now' merged with an innumerable number of the 'selfs' gone by which his memory confronted as 'strangers' and even enemies of the self he projected as his moral show-case. How many of those 'selfs' would he have liked to expunge from his memory. How many of such 'selfs' would he have liked to push irretrievably into the abysmal depths of his subconscious mind and into oblivion.

He continued leaning back against the trunk of the tree, the tree with aerial roots like the columns of the temple of Jerusalem, with closed eyes. It was under this tree that he had fought one whole night as Jacob did with an angel who was God himself. Now he realized that the God he wrestled with and overcame was his false self, the builder of the house of craving and greed. He had vanquished the builder of the house of torments, of sufferings, of remorse, of regret, of shame. He had identified and overcome this self, this actor that had made him appear ceaselessly, incessantly, uninterruptedly and continuously on the ever changing stages and scenes of the countless dramas of his life.

How did you come to the realization of your false self, Lord? A questioner was asking.

On hearing this question his mind began to travel down the corridors of his memory. He was seeing the identities, the many 'selfs', that he had assumed on the stages of time. After a long pause he spoke.

You feel you are one and the same. You feel that you were, that you are and that you will be. From where does this feeling arise? It arises from your form, your form that is without substance, which is emptiness and which is void. Your self is the creation of that form. It is the mirage of a desert. It is a mirage that arises both in your conscious mind through thoughts and feelings as well as in your subconscious mind in dreams and other stirrings. Is this self one which you always embrace and hold fast to? Is it one which always does honour to you and maintains your dignity? That self should be something you would expect it to be without change and mutation: always steadfast and true.

But how often have you wished to dissociate yourself from this very 'self' you are clinging to? How often does your awareness confront you with a 'self' you want to break away from, to tear yourself away from? How often does your self confront you with events and happenings that make you ashamed of yourself? In the stillness of this awareness, how often do you cry out, no, that was not me? No, I wish that had never been me? No, I wish that I had been other than what I was?

How often have you searched to hide your face before situations in which your self brought you shame, regret, remorse, suffering and sorrow? How much have you wished that your identity, your self had been different, that it had taken you through life without such shame and sorrow. How much have you wished to be a 'self' that only brought you joy and happiness? How often have you confronted these two 'selfs', these two identities, the one that is you, and the one you would have liked to be, the one you would have gladly separated yourself from, and the one you would have gladly identified yourself with, the one that was ugly and the one that was beautiful?

And did you know that this beautiful self was always within you, waiting to be discovered. How often have you yearned for this permanent, unchanging 'Self'? The day you achieve that transformation into the real 'Self' that you are, the 'Self' that is the Lord of self, that day you will say: *Late have I loved you, O Beauty ever ancient, ever new, late have I loved you! You were within me, but I was outside, and it was there that I searched for you. In my unloveliness I plunged into the lovely things which you created. You were with me, but I was not with you. Created things kept me from you; yet if they had not been in you, they would have not been at all. You called, you shouted, and you broke through my deafness. You flashed, you shone, and you dispelled my blindness. You breathed your fragrance on me; I drew in breath and now I pant for you. I have tasted you, now I hunger and thirst for more. You touched me, and I burned for your peace. For Thine is the kingdom, the power and the glory for ever.*

He had realized that this self, this actor, this stage identity was a fake, a fraud, the untruth, ir-reality and falsehood of a deluded mind. This void and emptiness he had assumed to be his identity and his self, this self that had been fed by the fire of craving and greed. This fire within him had now been blown out. He was finally free. That realization had made him to cry out with all the energy, power and strength of his body: *And a vision of insight arose in me thus: Unshakable is the deliverance of my heart.* The realization that dawned on me was that I was not the creation of my form. My SELF realization would never more be dependent on the forms through which that SELF would manifest itself. That SELF would henceforth assume whatever form it deemed necessary to reveal itself as the light that is the life of men.

Now what? he had asked himself. Could I leave this void and emptiness like Enoch did by letting myself be 'taken up to heaven'? Could I leave this void and emptiness as Elijah did, being 'carried away in a fiery chariot'? Could I be like Melchizedek who appeared on the scene from nowhere and then disappeared from it without leaving any trace behind? All he saw around him were his fellow human beings blinded and made sightless by craving and greed. They were crying out to him: *Lord that I may see.* How can I leave them and go? He asked. If I the seer forsake the blind that cry out to me, will they not plunge to their destruction? How can I leave them and go? How can I leave them and go?

~~~ ~~~ ~~~

CHAPTER 31 - AN UNEXPECTED MEETING

✀ ✀   ✀ ✀

He closed his eyes again as if trying to erase the dream that had engrossed him. It was then that he heard the sound of feet approaching him softly and discretely. As he half opened his eyes what he saw was an approaching form. He kept his eyes on the form as it came nearer. It was a woman. She held two baskets in her arms. While in his presence, she knelt down, placed the baskets on the ground near his feet and worshiped him.

Eat and drink Lord, she said. *You are hungry and thirsty and you have a long journey before you. Forty days have now elapsed since you began your fast.*

Forty days? he asked with a weak quivering and incredulous voice

Yes, forty days, she replied in a voice replete with tenderness.

The words 'forty days' set his mind in a whirl. He recalled how as Moses he had fasted on the mountain for forty days on two occasions. As Jesus he had yet again emerged from a forty days fast in the wilderness.

Then she looked up and as their eyes met sudden recognition dawned on him. Just as he was about to call her by her name she stopped him by placing her forefinger against her lips. Of a sudden their memories had come alive. She recalled their conversation of a day gone which was transpiring before their very eyes. She was telling him: *We are the actors on the stage of dreams.* Even as she spoke Adam, her Adam was being metamorphosed before her eyes, just as she. With each metamorphosis did also the time, clime and environment undergo the corresponding change. Colours, hues and landscape as well as personal features, qualities, endowments right down to every vestige of clothing were in the process of mutation.

For a fleeting moment she saw him seated, just as he now was, under a tree. That tree which was once the tree of the knowledge of good and evil had itself been transformed for a fleeting moment into the Tree of Enlightenment. The man seated under that tree, the primordial man, was the love of her life. His eyes were half closed and directed towards the earth while she knelt before him with two bowls of food in her hands. From the depths of the earth to the uppermost heights of the heavenly vault his teaching was resonating.

Becoming and re-becoming is the nature of all phenomena. From sunrise to sunset, the day is ever changing, never static. It rises seemingly energized but then it wanes into deep slumber until it re-becomes with the next sunrise. No two days are identical. The birth and death of each day illustrates the movement of the wheel of becoming, symbol of eternal cyclic existence. Differences of time and space are illusions of the human mind, of the form that is an actor on the stage of dreams.

Indeed only the conscious power of which each of us is a manifestation is real and true, Everything else is an illusion including our forms and their stage generated identities, our 'selfs'.

You recognized me for who I am, she told him. You have long since learned not to confuse my changing forms and names with my unchanging identity. Yet different times and different climes with their concurrent socio-religious networks determine their own values and impose their own dictates. They must be respected. So call me Sujatha for now, yes, Sujatha. The form receded as if borne by the wind and vanished in the distance. He had his eyes fixed on the horizon as if expecting her to reappear.

What he next heard was a voice. You know who she is, the voice said. It can only be her and no other. Forms change, as do names. So also with cultures and religions. You saw her and recognized her, the primordial woman. She had brought you food and drink. Where you are is only a stage in your journey to the holy mountain. Call it Horeb or whatever you wish, but it is a place in your mind, and there the Lord will manifest himself to you. There she too will reveal herself to you in her true nature. So eat, drink, regain your force and move on.

When he regained his previous awareness the speaker had stopped his discourse and the audience was dispersing.

CHAPTER 32 - WHAT OTHERS THOUGHT OF HIM

Now he was standing facing his disciples and asking them: *Who do people say I am*?

They replied, Some say John the Baptist; others say Elijah; and still others, Jeremiah or one of the prophets.

But what about you? he asked. *Who do you say I am*?

Simon Peter answered, You are the Messiah, the Son of the living God.

Then, as he was wont to regularly do when a debate arose within himself, he left them and proceeded deep into the desert to be alone. His two questions to his disciples kept repeating themselves within his mind: *who do people say I am? Who do you say I am?* With his gift of clairvoyance he did not have to look into a too distant future to know the answer. The variety and scale of responses to that question defied imagination itself. What occurred in his regard after his resurrection left many unanswered questions. He appeared to some and disappeared from their sight in no time. What those privileged with such apparitions engaged in were reconstructions of his person from details they thought existed in their memories. They were linked to sound, gestures and tactile sensations. He was a reconstruction of their minds.

Now who was this reconstructed individual? Was it the real Jesus of history? Was it a myth? Was it the devil appearing as an angel of light? The reconstruction varied with the individuals engaged in that endeavour, yet they agreed that it was he and no other. How could that be? How could he be the identical product of thought processes that differed the one from the other? His mind was in a whirl. He was thinking of how the monotheistic God of the Torah was splintered and fragmented according to the religious, historical, political and social vicissitudes of a nation, and assumed characters that were not only deviations from that ideology but even totally contradictory in nature. That would also be his own destiny, because time and tide, the real ruler of the human mind was no respecter of persons, by whatever name one called them.

His vision now spanned the totality of time. What he saw was a Jesus become a lump of clay in the hands of his believers, and molded into forms of their choice, forms that catered to their self-indulgence, their religious desires, and their religious addictions. In this they were aided and abetted by pre-fabricated structures, paid pastors, church services, moving sermons, breath-taking ceremonials and hypnotic rituals, all in the name of faith. Such a faith can only be the entrance door to the murky maze of the occult lit only by the delusioned self.

Thereafter, Jesus saw himself become the object of a cult, venerated as a cosmic divinity. Others would only see him as a teacher and preacher of the coming Kingdom of God. For others, he would be the figure of a descending-ascending redeemer from heaven. He would also don the mantle of the divine 'word', a concept of Greek philosophy. There would also be the veneration of his person as the heavenly high priest: whether as a servant or child of God. There would be also those who would consider him as a part of the Godhead.

How many other forms of "Jesus" did not survive in extant documents is impossible to tell. But divergent groups and disciples all over the civilized world of that time preached an unspecified number of Jesus figures so different from one another: so different that each called the other an agent of Satan. All this fragmentation and breakup of Jesus into a multitude of component parts is an unprecedented phenomenon, and even more, each of these component parts seemed blissfully unaware of the others.

How can such a Jesus be me? His distracted mind was now querying. There has never been anyone more radical, confrontational and disruptive to the commonly held habits and doctrines of religion than me. I did not place any hope in politics, nor did I spend his time criticizing other religions; rather, I confronted, challenged and presented a better alternative to my own religion. My purpose in life was to end formal religion, and inspire mankind to live a life of faith in a new and selfless way, a way of the Spirit. That is why I declared to the Samaritan woman at the well, that a time will come when *God will no more be worshipped in sanctuaries wherever they be located, and in temples.* I was ushering in a time when *God will be worshipped only in Spirit and in Truth.*

And now the spirit, the one that blows on what or on whom it will and where it will was on him. He saw himself wandering within a temple among thousands of devotees of various cultures and civilizations. They were being guided through the different sanctuaries and altars by a priest of the temple. He was describing to them each and every statue. They were of all forms and shapes and were described as being the manifestations of the one God.

The guide was saying, 'these are Gods who have manifested themselves in the course of human history in many civilizations of mankind. This God here was born of a virgin. The birth of this God was heralded by a star. This one received the homage of wise men come from afar, while the one there had his birth announced by choirs of angels. This statue represents the God who raised people from the dead, and the other one there, walked over the waters and multiplied bread. The one you see on the other side rose from the dead and appeared to a woman devotee. That one walked through closed doors and surprised his disciples. The one over there ascended into heaven and was lost in the clouds.

Stunned by what he was seeing, he asked: What I see before me is a pantheon.

So it is. The reply seemed to him to come from over the horizon.

Then who am I? Am I one among these ones, or are these ones other forms of the one that I am? I feel as if it is I, the temple; I, the pantheon. Then who is the one God: the one who is the one and the only one with no one else beside him?

The answer was immediate. There was one God, so to say, at one time. But paradoxically, that was before time began. That God was one, which in turn means he was alone. It is not good even for God to be alone. Hence the infinite and eternal God had a dream as infinite and eternal as himself. That dream was to don human flesh and blood and enter the domain of time and space. The subsequent events prove it. He looked into the mirror of his consciousness called the waters. What he saw was his image and likeness. He was seeing himself as man and woman: as word and wisdom; as glory and power. The other, his image and likeness, could not be as he was, for if it had, then it too would have been alone. It had to be really other, really different. It had to manifest himself as he and not he: as the one and the other. Now he was no more alone.

So did God in his infinite wisdom, put on the face of time appearing as splintered and fragmented, for the face of time is a changing face. It rises and ceases. Now what rises and ceases is never the same. So did the one God, the THEOS, become the many Gods, the PAN-THEON or the changing faces of God. With those words the vision ended.

What he confronted now was another question. What would I tell the followers regarding these multiplications and adaptations of my person and identity? That query he could not evade.

And so he donned the personality of an ascetic of a far away time and clime and taught: "*Do not believe in any teaching attributed to me simply because you have heard it. Do not believe in it simply because it is spoken and rumored by many. Do not believe in it simply because it is found written in your religious books, the scriptures or any other. Do not believe in it merely on the authority of your teachers and elders. Do not believe in traditions that concern me because they have been handed down for many generations. But after observation and analysis of my doctrine, when you find that anything agrees with your aspirations and is conducive to the good, the benefit and the happiness of one and all, then accept it, enter into it, abide in it, and live up to it."*

Then in one sweeping vision he saw the ones of the earth that were hungry, that were thirsty, that were poor and helpless, that were in prison, that suffered for the cause of justice. He saw them all. And now all their forms, the forms they had assumed in all the unfolding of time and space were merging and blending together into one, and that one was he.

See, he said, and his voice reached the four corners of the earth, *See… that is me. Do not search for me in statues, in pantheons. Do not search for me in temples. Do not search for me in sanctuaries and in holy places. Do not grope towards the light through cults, rites and liturgies. I am the other, the one in front of you, the one who stands before you. I am that other, the one who is hungry, thirsty, poor and helpless. I am the one in prison, the one that suffers injustice. This is the supreme teaching I impart to you. No other matters. What you do to the least of my brethren, you do to me. This is the ultimate reality: this is the ultimate truth. That and that only is the way, the truth and the life: there is no other.*

CHAPTER 33 - WHAT HE THOUGHT OF HIMSELF

And then the question turned inwards. He was now asking himself: *who do I think that I am?* Then of a sudden there propped up before his eyes the images of a burning bush and of himself transfigured flanked by Moses and Elijah. At the next instant Moses was alone confronting the burning bush. He followed the conversation that ensued and the divine imperative that Moses face the Pharaoh demanding the release of the enslaved Israelites. Moses was asking God to reveal his name so that he could answer the inevitable question of the Pharaoh. Suddenly he felt himself ablaze like the sun with flames sprouting out of him and around him, and he heard himself say: *I am who am.*

That moment of transfiguration and transformation had vanished. The power and the glory with which he had felt himself endowed was gone, leaving behind a serious question. *What was this particular experience that I had undergone? A dream? A vision?* The question was all the more pertinent because there was not a trace of the desert into which he had advanced leaving his disciples behind him. He found himself in a luscious garden he felt he had known before.

That is right, a voice was telling him, you are indeed in a garden, the one in which you came into being: Eden, or more simply, paradise.

He looked around searching for the place from which the voice emanated.

Look ahead and not behind, the same voice was now telling him.

As he turned his head forward, he saw that he was facing a tree from which a quivering slimy form was stretching itself outward. It had an apple in its mouth. It was however not being offered to him, but to someone standing by his side. He looked sideways and saw a woman.

Now it all came back to him. That was she, the woman who had surged out of his subconscious mind taking the form that had been his eternal dream, that refused to leave him even in his deepest sleep. He was the human form of God's eternal word. It was she that filled that eternal word with wisdom. Now what is a word without wisdom? They were both the human expression of the Infinite, Eternal and Everlasting God.

Now that God had taken human form appearing as male and female, he could not continue to remain hidden. He could not continue to be unfathomable and inaccessible to the human mind. God had now entered the realm of time and space. Time and space would be his tabernacle among men. Time and space perceived as the human form would now form the pages through which God would be revealed to the world. Human forms would continue their apparent existences as the one and the other, but the divine consciousness would be the ground of their being and their ultimate destiny. This truth, his truth, the one which pervaded his consciousness, throbbed with every heartbeat, and seemed to saturate every drop of his blood. That truth was his body. That truth was his blood. That truth was his life. He had no escape from it.

I know what you are thinking, he heard the serpent say. But all that is beside the point. The point simply is: what is the nature of all that thought? Is it divine or is it human? I personally think you have a deluded mind. Ask yourself the simple question, namely, are you a human being or are you a manifestation of God? If you are fully human as you seem to be, then how can your human mind unravel the nature, the mind, the will and the life of God? If your thoughts are human thoughts there is nothing divine about them. The divine is over and above you. It is beyond you. If you are human, God is in no way committed to your thoughts, your words and your deeds. You can think, say and do whatever you wish, but they can have no other impact other than within your world. So too it is therefore with what others think of you. What they think of you colour their personal world and nothing more.

The crucial question however remains, and that regards your belief, continued the serpent. If you believe that what others say about you and what you think of yourself is of divine origin, then such a belief as well as its consequences are totally personal and subjective. Naturally, you are free to think whatever you wish regarding your own self, so as others are free to think as they wish about you.

Now he was alone. All around him stretched the desert sands and their undulating dunes. His mind was anguished, so anguished that drops of blood appeared on the surface of his skin in place of sweat. He grappled with the issue. Was he divine in human form? Or was he purely human? Was his sense of divinity just a belief, an unshakable thought, or was it a reality? Was it his nature? Had divinity seeped into his flesh and blood impregnating his mind and his will?

CHAPTER 34 - DESERT AND MIRAGES

✘✘　✘✘

Was divinity his nature? Had divinity seeped into his flesh and blood impregnating his mind and his will? Had this question any significance or was it a path leading to a mirage? The desert had always been his living space and the mountain heights his audience hall with God. But the desert had mirages. They were gardens associated with the crucial episodes of his life. One such mirage was the garden of Eden. Then there were others as well. There was the garden of Gethsamanee, the eerie rocky space that was Golgotha, and the garden that contained the resting places of the dead. These were all mirages or fruits of the desert. The word 'fruit' produced a strange resonance in his mind.

Mirages were not just consolations or torments that the desert offered to a weary traveler, they were the physical revelations about the desert traveler's state of mind. They were real as long as they were seen from a distance. But on entering into them, they literally dissolved within the body so intent on enjoying the promises they held out. It was always the body that paid the price for the effusions of the mind. Just as the spaces were transformed at the behest of the mind, the body too was susceptible to undergo changes within those very spaces. Once so transformed his body transcended time and assumed an ethereal dimension.

Troubled by the question that pursued him, he saw himself being flanked by the ones supposedly gone before, one of whom was expected to come after. On his right was Moses, while on his left was Elijah. They were poised on the ladder of Jacob with supraterrestrial beings moving up and down. Poised over and above the ladder was he who is, who was saying: *I am the Lord*.

Jesus, said the voice, your striving must be to blend and merge with what is over and above. Whenever and wherever you place yourself within a so called now, you will always dream of a past and a future. There is no present without a past and a future. This stands to reason. If you consider the present without a past and future, such a present would be as a dream ladder to the over and above, such an endeavour would stand not to reason but to imagination. Imagination is the unfolding of the dream.

In the garden of paradise called Eden, you as Adam and Miriam as Eve made a choice, to love one another for ever and to stay as the strength and support of your progeny also for ever. You are the ladder that will lead them from the ir-reality of the passing present to the hidden, unknown and unseen over and above, which is the truth that no eye hath seen, no ear hath heard and no human heart hath conceived. Jesus, when you don the mantle of time, you are a man limited and restricted to a particular space with all its dictates of history, of law and of customs and usages.

Find refuge in your dreams to escape the tyranny of time. Time and space do not permit transformations and transfigurations but dreams do. There is no reality in time and space. A present that fades into the past and opens out into a future is not real, it is ir-real. It is a passing scene without substance. The more you look on this ir-reality for what it is, a dream, the more it will transform and transfigure you. The dream will be to you as a Mount Sinai and a Mount Horeb. It will be to you as the ladder of Jacob. Only then can you hope to glimpse an over and above, a beyond, which is the truth. Only then will you discover the identity of he who is, who was saying: *I am the Lord.*

It was as if the spirit was hovering over the eternal waters. Out of it arose forms which were all his own. Each of them was endowed with a distinct identity, that made them look distinct from one another just as are succeeding waves. As long as the mind was hypnotized by the waves, what it saw was the many. Yet they were the manifestation of the one ocean. *That is you that one: the ground of all that appears and disappears on the stage of life.* The voice within him was clear and without any ambiguity.

CHAPTER 35 – WHERE IS GOD?

He sat on the desert sands with the pyramids fully in the field of his vision. With his Jewish background and knowledge of the Torah what appeared before his eyes were dumbfounding. The scene was changing between the Mount Sinai, also called Mount Horeb, and the unimaginable ladder that stretched from earth to heaven. With the change of scene, he himself had undergone a change of form and identity. Everything that was taking place was happening within one unified field of vision and experience.

He was now walking in the desert. He felt an unbearable heat during the day and a freezing cold by night. He felt his feet sink in the soft sands which impeded his movements. The wind was blowing against the sand dunes, turning them into undulating mounds that were being endlessly displaced. He was without a stable point of reference by which to gauge his advance in the desert. The moving sands gave him the feeling that he was not going anywhere but stamping his feet in the same place in the manner of a pantomimist. It was as if he was embedded in space and that time itself had come to a standstill. This strange situation made him experience the journey as a march inwards into the spaces of his mind.

With that sensation he had the distinct impression that he was crossing the boundaries of his senses. Progressively he entered the realms of his mind and stepped over the frontiers of his reasoning processes. Now he was walking through the domain of his memory into an imaginary world. It was then he felt himself climbing upwards. He was scaling what appeared to him to be a spiritual mountain. He now heard cries surging upwards from below. Looking downwards, he saw an immense multitude that was following his every movement. Then piercing through the cold air, he heard a feminine voice shout out: *Moses*. He recognized that voice as being that of his companion Miriam.

That voice plucked him away from his mountain perch and was wafting him into a greenish plane through which a mighty river flowed. The Nile, he shouted into the four winds: the Nile. And there among the bulrushes he saw a floating object, a basket made of reeds that contained the fragile form of an infant. And not far from there, hiding behind a juniper tree was a slight figure of a girl. *Miriam*, he cried out, *Miriam*. He wanted to reach out to her when it dawned on him that his hands were grasping a rocky outcrop and realized that he had not left the mountain and that it was his spirit that was making him relive his out of body experiences. He continued his climb though his legs were refusing to carry him further, and his benumbed fingers were losing their hold on the rocky projections that served him as supports.

Soon he was enveloped in a thick cloud and had lost his bearings. He only knew he was in the desert and climbing a very high mountain. An intense sense of loneliness invaded him. He felt cut off completely from the sensory world in which he was engulfed. As he progressed step by step upwards, the steep slope on which he was perched, the feeling dawned on him that he was on a ladder. Cut off from everything around him by the thick cloud which became denser and denser, he felt like someone who was falling asleep. What occurred next took him by surprise. He felt a hand in his hand. That hand was soft, warm and comforting. No word was spoken. But at no moment did he feel insecure.

Then he felt himself gently ushered into what appeared to be a cave. Once again he was alone. Weighed down by an unusual fatigue, he lay down on the floor of the rocky refuge and fell into a deep sleep. All of a sudden everything within him seemed to light up with an ethereal light. His state of mind presented to him all the attributes of a dream.

Who am I? Hovered the question in his mind. Am I Moses, Elijah, Jacob, Jeremiah or Ezechiel? Am I the one or the other of them?

And why not all of them within one consciousness, a voice interjected. Could not each and every one of them reproduce the words God uttered with regard to Jeremiah: *Before I formed you in the womb I knew you, before you were born I set you apart; I appointed you as a prophet to the nations*? The word 'YOU' God used, did it designate each individually or did it designate all as one?

The same voice continued and said: what you are going to witness now is the presence of God. The voice continued:

Go forth and stand on the mountain ledge and watch. What he experienced would have terrified any mortal being and brought about his death.

Where are you Lord? he screamed into the great void that had opened before him.

I am passing by, an echo seemed to come from afar. You will not see me for no one can look on my face and live.

And, behold, the LORD was passing by! And a great and strong wind was tearing the mountains apart, making pieces of rock break up and fly like projectiles; but the LORD was not in the wind. And after the wind, a ground shattering earthquake made the mountain tremble and shake like a sand dune caught in a violent desert storm, but the LORD was not in the earthquake. After the earthquake a devastating fire took over, and the mountain was burning with huge flames leaping skyward, but the LORD was not in the fire.

After the fire a sound of a gentle blowing caressed his face and body. That gentle breeze he realized was the stirring of his mind and heart attuned to the silence and the stillness of the Infinite. The voice then told him: *do not search for God in the histrionics of nature, in the tearing of the mountains, in ground shattering earthquakes, in devastating fires. God is the gentle breeze, the gentle wind within you with no wherefrom and whereto. But what it is you will know. You will soon know that what IS is word and wisdom, glory and power.*

CHAPTER 36 - VISION OF GLORY

✠✠ ✠✠

What followed now bewildered him. He saw a ladder stretching from where he stood towards the heavens and rest on a support that appeared to him to be far beyond the stars and the heavenly bodies. He was now climbing without the slightest trace of tiredness. He found himself climbing at an astounding speed that totally surprised him. He felt his body become flesh-less and weightless as he ascended into the heavens, taking the appearance of a luminous form. He had been transfigured, and to his utter astonishment, he was being led by Moses and Elijah. Fortified by their presence and sensing what was to come, he rasied his armes to the heavens and cried out with a loud voice: *Father, I glorified You on the earth, having accomplished the work which You have given Me to do. Now, Father, glorify Me together with Yourself, with the glory which I had with You before the world was.*

He had practically reached the extreme end of the ladder above the firmament, when he saw the likeness of a throne. On this throne was the appearance of a man who sat upon it. Dazzling rays were being emitted on every side of the throne. He who sat on the throne was clothed in the sun. By his side on the throne sat a female form, a woman.

Suddenly the stupefaction that invaded his being seemed to subside with the dawn of awareness that the figure on the throne was he.

At that moment a voice reverberated through the heavenly vault: *in the beginning was the Word and the Word was with God and the Word was God. All things were made by him; and without him was not any thing made that was made. In him is life; and the life is the light of men. Behold him now, the Word, my beloved son.* And then he felt the gentle hand of the woman on his own. They looked at each other and recognition dawned. *I am Wisdom,* she said. *Out of my fullness proceeds the Word. I Wisdom and you Word are one. You are son and bridegroom while I am mother and bride. In us resides the Godhead as parent, spouse and companion, for such is the nature of God.*

Their consciousness and awareness was one and the same. It was infinite, eternal and immortal. Out of it, as out of the eternal waters, life was flowing and taking shape before their eyes. Within their consciousness the earth and the heavens were coming into being. The oceans were throbbing with life, and their waves placidly beating against the white sands. The great mountains were surging upwards and the tips of their pyramidal forms were pointing towards the heavens. Their consciousness, lit up with heavenly light, had become the light of men and of the universe.

Now the entire creation seemed to be dancing in the throes of ecstasy, and acclaiming the one Godhead appearing as man and woman. The entire creation was exulting with one voice that rang out from the four corners of the unfathomable universe and into the depthless depths of time without end: *Thou art That.* That divine consciousness, the enlivener and sustainer of all creation, was proclaiming its kingdom, its power and its glory with the sacred and solemn words: *I am who am.*

As he emerged from his ecstatic vision, he saw scenes succeeding one another in the spaces of his mind. Now he was telling a hostile crowd: *Your father Abraham rejoiced to see My day, and he saw it and was glad.* So the Jews said to Him, You are not yet fifty years old, and have You seen Abraham? He heard himself telling them: *Truly, truly, I say to you, before Abraham was born, I am.* He was seeing them picking up stones to throw at Him. Yet again He was witnessing a courtroom scene. He had been brought before the great ones of the earth who were asking him the question that would bring about his condemnation and death.

The question was: *are you a king?*

His answer was: you have said it. And you will see the son of man coming down on the clouds of heaven to judge the living and the dead.

Scenes also shot up in his mind of his excruciating death and burial. He saw his spirit in a manner that recalled the journey of the pharaohs and of the heroes of mythology, descend to the netherworld, kingdom of the shadows of the dead, to open to them the portals of immortality and join Hades with Heaven in one infinite, eternal and everlasting kingdom that is the divine consciousness. That kingdom was the heritage of the children of God, from which none would be excluded whatever be their race, religion and civilization.

~~~ ~~~ ~~~

CHAPTER 37 - LIGHT THAT IS LIFE

After a moment of reverie and with the previous experience still throbbing in his mind, he was reviewing the first verses of the book of Genesis as they appeared in the Torah. In the beginning God created the heavens and the earth. Now the earth was formless and empty. Darkness was over the surface of the deep, and the spirit of God was hovering over the waters. And God said, *"let there be light, and there was light. Now that light was the light of men"*.

What was that light? The question sprang up within him.

It was life. So precious was that light, the life of men, that civilizations will depict the waters or the oceans as the scene of an unending tussle between gods and demons, ever engaged in churning the milky ocean to extract the elixir that is life, which is the hope of immortality. Since the moment when God said 'let there be light, the life of men', so impregnating the womb that is mother earth, life will never become extinct. And so, no one will ever die.

Then what is it we call death?

Death is a deep sleep. Now deep sleep is what comes closest to touching the above and the beyond, the confines of the great divide or eternity. In sleep one does not feel and therefore know that time is passing. Yet the effects of passing time appear on the canvas that is the physical form or the body. When death intervenes the body decays and becomes dust. Yet consciousness which is light and the life of men remains. It will remain in each particle of the dust into which the body has disintergrated. That dust will be churned anew in the womb of the waters the ever moving spheres of earth through its surrogate form that is woman, and a new form will arise. It will have the same consciousness but not the same sense of identity, because the scene or the stage of life would have changed.

While all this transpired within him, suddenly a large space opened up in front of him. He was seeing a vagabond preacher, a form which he identified as being himself, walking in an open space, followed by a large gathering keenly intent on every word that gushed from his mouth. It was then that he heard the voice that cried out to him: *Lord that I may see*. The scene he had lived through under the exotic tree was all being replayed in that poignant cry: *Lord that I may see*. He was looking in the direction of the voice and seeing the blind man who was pleading with him for the restoration of his sight. Cured by his touch and interrogated by his enemies the man limited his explanation to the one phrase that mattered; *all I know is that I whereas I was blind, now I see*.

Now he was listening as the disciples asked him: *who was it who sinned for this man to be born blind? Was it he himself or his parents?* His vision was directed towards horizons beyond the pale of the minds of his followers. Of what interest was it to know who had sinned? And did it finally matter?

Amidst the din and clatter around him, he heard his voice emanating from under that very same tree, a voice which was saying: if any one of you is struck by an arrow deeply embedded in your flesh, how would you react? Would you be asking all and sundry that came upon the scene: who shot me? Where was he hiding? Why did he do it? Why me and not another? These questions would all be besides the point. All he would ask is: please remove this arrow from my body. That was what was foremost in the mind of the poor blind man.

His cry was not about the circumstances of his condition, but the cure: *Lord, that I may see.* What he had seen and heard that night was a vision and a revelation. Blindness was the absence of light. Blindness was living in darkness. But was the blindness of that man the only blindness that beset mankind? Could one experience darkness with eyes open to the sunlight? Could there be blindness through refusal to see the light? To be blind was to be in the dark.

Such a blinding darkness a woman experienced, a woman who had stood under the cross and seen him die. She had followed his body to the tomb. When everyone had departed she had remained, her head against the boulder that shut the entrance to that tomb. Her anguished questions were: where are you my Jesus? If you are nowhere, then why am I here? What am I suffering for? If there be no Jesus, then I cannot be what I think I am, the woman who took form and spirit out of his body Then I am a fake, a living lie. I do not want just to believe that you live, but know that you live in me, and I in you. and yet the reality of darkness and coldness and emptiness is so great that that hope is an illusion. The emptiness that I feel is like sharp knives being plunged into my very spirit. I am in total darkness,

Jesus, why have you forsaken me? Your silence has plunged me in darkness. Jesus if you are dead, then my soul too is dead and my body is as a mummified body waiting for your return. Come alive Jesus and let me rise again body and soul with you. It was out of you that I issued forth. Without you I am what the earth was at the beginning: void and formless. Without you there is no way, no truth, and no life. Come back. Hover over me. Give me the light that is your life. Lord, that I may see the light and rise to a new life with you.

She was undergoing the dark night of her soul. But unknown to her Jesus was himself undergoing such a night. His soul had left his body. It was wandering in the darkness. It was wandering through subterranean corridors as a bodyless shadow, trying to remember his identity. His wanderings would take eons but appear as a day, because whatever one calls the passage of time, one can only experience it as the present, as the here and as the now. Guided by the dictates of his memory he would return to where his body lay. But that would not be enough. He would have to see and experience his other half.

He had returned to his body, pushed open the boulder of the tomb and emerged into the light. He saw what was around him were forms with no identities. As such, being outside the web of earthly life, he had no identity himself, and then it happened. He saw a woman who was asking him where he had laid the body of her Lord. In the twinkling of an eye, he recognized her voice and her form.

That voice and that form had pulled him within the web of life, the web of identities, of others as well as his own. *Miriam*, he shouted to the four winds. *Miriam, it is me, Miriam,* he said repeating the name and addressing the form, the womanly form out of which his identity had reemerged. *Miriam, whereas I was blind, now I see.* It was then and only then that she came to life. It was once again the voice that led her to the identification of the form.

Master, she cried out, flinging herself at his feet and embracing his legs.

CHAPTER 38 - THE GLORY OF GOD

His mission was now filled with clarity. It was to cure the blind and hear their explosion of joy in the triumphant cry: *whereas I was blind, now I see*. And what would they see? What they would see is the glory of God: the light that is the life of men. Without that light humanity is blind.

The question his disciples asked him still assailed his mind. *Why was this man born blind? Who had sinned? He himself or his parents?* Or another? At this moment his mind was flooded with light.

He heard himself answer: not he nor his parents nor any other. It so was so that the glory of God be revealed.

How can a poor man's blindness reveal the glory of Almighty, Everlasting and Infinite God? The questions persisted.

Now silence prevailed within him and around him. Do you understand what you are saying? he asked. Can you conceive this God? Can you understand him? Can you circumscribe him within your mnd? God is all that you are not: almighty. everlasting, and infinite. If so, how can you know and understand the glory of God? Have you not read in the sacred scriptures that no one can see God and live? But you have also read that nothing is impossible to God.

God's glory can be known, understood and seen only by those to whom God deigns to reveal Himself.

The glory of God is divine light: eternal, infinite, everlasting light. It is the lighty of the beatific vision of God himself. It is the light that is the divine consciousness: the light by which God knows himself. Those who are lit up by the glory of God SEE GOD. Those who are lit with the glory of God, do not see a blind man before them. They do not see the defects and deformities of birth or man imposed impurities in others What they see is God in human form.

His vision was now extending to the ends of the earth. He was seeing a frail woman who had made the slums and the most impoverished and destitute parts of Calcutta her home. People were shouting to her. They called her 'Mother'...they called her 'Teresa'. To her God had revealed his glory. Her vision filled with the divine light that is the glory of God did not see anyone as being blind. She did not see anyone as old, decrepid, filled with sores and stench. She did not see anyone as impure and untouchable. The miserable of the earth, the ones condemned by society on whatever ground, be it utter poverty, be it the most loathsome diseases leprosy or other, or be the vileness and impurity ascribed to untouchability, those whom society considered as being darkness personified and relegated to live in cemeteries she saw them in the eternal, infinite and everlasting light that is God's glory. In that divine light what she saw in them was God in human form. She saw them clothed in God's glory.

Lover, mother and companion, these are the three vocations of womanhood that the act of creation bestowed on earth and its surrogate human forms. All this was the work of God *who knows the heart of man and what is in man.* The primary and primordial yearning of man is for love. All these yearnings of man are incorporated and come to fruition in the form of a woman. *He shall therefore leave all and cling to the woman, and they shall be one flesh.*

Miriam, he said the name gushing out from his heart. *Thou art THAT.* What does it matter which name you bear. The people of the slums and gutters of Calcutta called you 'Teresa'. You are the primordial woman. It is you the triune goddess taking the form that times and climes demand. And so I will follow you, myself taking the forms that the unfolding of time confer on me. My sole aim is to cling to you and be one with you, because such is the will of God.

Suddenly silence prevailed. The soul of the Master had taken flight. He was watching the endless waves churning out of the ocean of time the deepest yearning of humanity, the yearning for the Godhead to be revealed as spouse, mother and companion. Yet what imposed itself in the field of his vision were religious societies rising up and consolidating themselves as bastions of male dominance specifically through appropriation of the function of the priesthood, the intermediary between earth and heaven. Yet they too had to bow before the irrepressible dictate which was the yearning for the Mother Goddess.

He saw the passing scene which was the earth replete from end to end with sanctuaries, statues, every imaginable place of worship dedicated to the Mother goddess. Even when the term 'goddess' had to to be masked and camouflaged under endless susbterfuges yet that human yearning was crying out to the heavens to be appeased. And so the mother goddess found its way into the sacrosanct realm of the mystery that is the Godhead through being proclaimed 'Mother of God' and 'Queen of the heavens'.

Then emerging from his silence, he spoke. THAT which was before the beginning could only exist as POWER, as SHAKTHI. The nature of THAT is one of power. It is the power that brings forth, that sustains, and that takes back to itself and regenerates. That power is TRIUNE manifesting itself as the mother that gives birth, that feeds, and that receives back into her arms. That power reveals itself as companion who accompanies, supports, and sustains. That power reveals itself as lover impregnated with and bearing in her womb the eternal seed of the light that is life.

CHAPTER 39 - BACK TO THE LAND OF BIRTH

That experience was a decisive moment of his life. It had inculcated in him a sense of the urgency of his mission.

Now in what lies your mission? his inner voice was asking him.

The reply seemed to come from afar: my mission is to do the will of my Father.

Just as God who is fullness and plenitude must reveal himself to be recognized, so too it is with his human manifestation. It is through the eruption of a volcano that one recognizes the power hidden in the bowels of the earth. It is through the eruption of a whirlpool that the ocean reveals the strength of its depths. So too the spirit has erupted within me and filled me with the divine consciousness of my mission which is to do the will of God.

Driven by the spirit he was now returning to a far away land that his people had practically recovered from the desert, a hard, dry and dusty land with houses in clay with hard material for roofing, and hard dusty streets along which men and woman in long robes and sandaled feet moved about relentlessly and uninterruptedly. It was a country that was visibly occupied by a foreign force. Soldiers with metal protections and wielding swords and daggers moved about menacingly, surveying everything and everyone on which their glance fell. The atmosphere was one of great hostility and mistrust. As his eyes skimmed the distance, he saw a band of men and women approaching. They walked slowly and their allure was so peaceful. In the center of the approaching crowd was a young man with a shaggy unshaven head of hair and an overgrown beard. He was the leader of the group.

Who is he? Someone asked

A Jew who left the country some eighteen hears ago and who has just returned. He is a preacher but not like the ones that we know and are used to. He does everything our society forbids people to do. He breaks all the rules, violates all the taboos, has no respect for authority, and is free with women. He preaches a different God, and inculcates a different set of values for the individual and for society.

But he has a big following. Why so?

Yes, all the outcasts of society, the underprivileged, the marginalized follow him.

From where has he learned these new doctrines and from where does he derive his great force to be a rebel? Where did he live during these long eighteen years?

In Egypt, was the answer

The ones learned in the scriptures remembered what had been prophesied: *Out of Egypt have I called my son.*

There was nothing new in the scriptures for him. He had the strange feeling that he had been there right through its unfolding. It was even more, he felt the entire story bursting out of him and claiming his attention. It was before him not as pages of a book turned by an invisible hand, but as a single and simple writing that contained it all and kept it ever present before his eyes. He not only knew it all, but saw, heard and felt it all as one single, all comprehensive happening. He felt that he had been before it, that he always was present during its occurrence, and that he would be there to the very end, even after it was all over and done with. He said: *I am the alpha and the omega, the beginning and the end. Indeed, before Abraham was, I am.*

CHAPTER 40 - GARDEN OF GETHSEMANE

Even while these thoughts and scenes were taking place within him he felt he was on the move, not by moving himself and of himself, but driven by a force within him and greater than himself. At times he felt the fullness of the spirit, but at other times also an immense sense of solitude and loneliness. Often he would sit on the ground and sink into a deep meditation. On such occasions the sense of time escaped him. How long he was so lost to the world he did not know, but on one such occasion his alert mind heard himself being called by a name that was not his. He heard himself being called: Adam. Adam,

Adam, the voice was repeatedly saying. He did not know whether the voice was coming from within him or from outside him. As he gently opened his eyes, he saw that a tree, an apple tree, had grown before his eyes. As his eyes progressively became accustomed to the light, he saw a moving form on the tree with its head stretched towards him. It was the serpent.

I followed you over the desert to the land of your birth. I searched for you and found you. *I recognized you*, the serpent said. You have changed form, but not your identity.

Then tell me who I am, he gently answered.

I called you by your name. Did you not hear me? I said: Adam.

There was one such person, he answered, but it was such a long time ago.

What is time? the serpent said. Nothing has passed. It is here and it is now. Certain minor details appear to have changed, he continued laughingly. Then it was such a beautiful and bounteous orchard. This here is still a desert. You remember where we first met Adam? By a tree. Trees have dominated your life Adam. First it was the tree of good and evil. Then it was the tree of immortality. Then other trees came on the scene. They were trees with the base of their canopies firmly grounded on the earth. They were the pyramids. They were the mountains, call them Sinai or Horeb or whatever. One tree even took the form of a ladder and stretched from the earth up to the heavens. You spent your life looking at trees, climbing them and eating out of their abundance.

But now another tree is beckoning to you. You refused my offer of joy in your youthful humanity, and forsook it for your dream of divinity. Soon you will regret your choice. You will soon find yourself in another garden. And there you will plead for your life. The cup of wine offered to you there will in no way be to your liking. You will even tell your maker: *let this chalice pass from me.*

The scene was now fading and he was once again sunk in a deep trance. He was indeed in another garden with the name Gethsemane. From a distance a vision was making itself manifest in the form of a tree, just as the serpent had stated. But dangling from that tree was not the form of the serpent offering him the fruit of the pleasures of the flesh, and the forms they metamorphosed into. What he saw dangling from that tree was the form of a crucified man. His blood was flowing like the wine of the marriage feast of Cana. The chalice he was being offered, however, contained vinegar and not wine.

At the same moment a woman was experiencing a vision, the vision of a garden. What she saw in it was a man afflicted with an unbearable sense of solitude, who was kneeling there in prayer. A voice was now pronouncing the name of the garden: it was Gethsemane. The man who was perspiring drops of blood in anticipation of an agonizing death was saying to God whom he called father: *not my will but thine be done, for thine is the kingdom, the power and the glory.*

What astounded her was that the man so praying caught in the throes of his agony was her man. How can this be, she asked herself. How can my man be duplicated and translocated into an unfathomably distant future, all in the batting of an eyelid, in an unchanging ever present here and now? Is the divine consciousness a theater in which the same actor reproduces himself simply by wearing a different mask? And then she saw a tree. *This tree is the tree of life,* she heard a voice say. *The form hanging from it is its fruit: the fruit that is his body and his blood.* The same voice continued to say: *eat of this fruit and you will not die, but you will live forever.* Then the scene vanished from her sight leaving her in a state of bewilderment.

The man nailed to the tree was in a state of delirium induced by the agony of his body. He found his mind resuscitating memories of the past, resurrecting them for review. He recalled a far-off day when he was led by his father, a very old and bearded man who held a newborn lamb round his neck. *A very old bearded man* he mused. *Just like the gardener-God of the garden of paradise my mother had dreamed about,* he said to himself. He had asked his father, *father, where are you taking me and why?*

We are going where God will that we go my son, and when we reach the place God will tell us why.

He then felt himself bound hands and feet, and gagged and blindfolded as well, lying on a long stone slab. He felt his father's hand holding him tightly by his hair distending his neck to the fullest. Then suddenly he felt his father releasing his hold on him and untying him. When he looked up, he saw his father beaming with suppressed jubilation. *God spoke to me,* he said. *He told me he will make you the father of a great nation. He told me he will dwell in your midst, till the end of time.*

From where did these scenes come from? He wondered. The bearded man whom he called father and the bearded man his mother called God and gardener of the garden of paradise. How did his mind conceive them? Your imagination, a voice within told him, just your imagination.

Just consider this Jesus, the same voice was saying. *Why are you dying?*

I am dying to show mankind that greater love hath no one but that he lay down his life for the other, so that he may have life eternal.

Oh really? But does this other know it? Does he care? Eternal life is a hope that springs eternal in every human breast. Your death is not going to add an iota to it. If mankind wants to kill someone to obtain eternal life, it will do so. And if mankind wants to resurrect someone to have eternal life, it will do so too. Furthermore it has been doing that all through the ages. So why you? The truth resulting from an awakening, an illumination, cannot be concentrated or petrified in one person. That is why the spirit breathed its awareness into forms that assumed your identity throughout the course of time.

He was hearing footsteps. Footsteps that approached out of the past, then the stillness of the present, and footsteps that receded, moving away from him into the future. It dawned on him that those footsteps were his own. His self was unmoving. His identity remained unmoved. The footsteps were those of forms searching his immobilized self, to merge with its identity. They were moving as if in circles around his immovable self. The wheel of forms was turning while his identity remained forever still.

He was brought to wakefulness by the voice. Jesus, the Spirit blows where it will. No one knows from where it comes and where it goes. We only see the effects. The wind does heap things together, but only temporarily. It scatters them again. What gets heaped, institutionalized and petrified, is not the working of the Spirit. Everything rises and ceases. Only the truth subsists. The greatest of all truths is love. Indeed all the commandments point out only to one truth: greater love hath no one but that he lay down his life for the other.

That is my mission. For that was I born.

Jesus, do you still remember what that High Priest said in your regard…when you were just twelve years old? Well, I will remind you. He said you are a dreamer. Now what are dreams but imagination.

Then is my imagination wrong? he asked from his invisible interlocutor.

What is right and wrong about mind-made truths? the voice asked

Are they true? he asked, changing the words.

If they are of relevance to you, then why not? was the reply.

So is it the relevance to me of what I conceive, be they ideas, words and forms whatever be their coatings and interconnections that make them the stuff out of which truth is made manifest?

As he asked this question the scene within the spaces of his mind were undergoing a change. The scene was being enacted on the battle field of Kurukshetra. He saw himself in the role of a warrior of a great epic. Behind him in the chariot on which he stood, bow and arrow in hand was his teacher and mentor. Is it right what I do? He was asking. It is your truth that must prevail, was the reply. Once that truth permeates your being there is no stepping back. So go and accomplish your mission however painful it be.

Quite so, the voice said, as if reading his thoughts.

What does all this mean? he asked.

Just this, that you are dying for your dream, the voice said, a dream that for you is so real and so true. Reality divorced from truth is no reality. But in you they are one.

CHAPTER 41 - BEGINNING THAT NEVER ENDS

That night he moved restlessly in his bed. He once again felt the presence of the devil.

You must die as all must die. Your death will be an excruciating and agonizing one. You willed it, did you not?

Yes I did, he confirmed.

Are you afraid to die?

He reflected a moment before answering. Not death the deep sleep but the pain. He saw himself on his knees on rocky ground praying to his father that he be spared the bitter chalice of that excruciating suffering.

He now found himself once more in a garden.

Where is the tree? he shouted, hoping the gardener would hear him.

Here it is, he heard a voice say, the voice of the gardener he had once known.

But it is not the same tree, he murmured with incredulity.

No was the answer. It is not the tree of good and evil. There is nothing more to know about it. Everyone is so engrossed in it, they do not see the other tree which however is the one very next to it and is the only one that matters.

Is it this tree? he asked, pointing to a tree with a different shape. It was a tree with a trunk and one horizontal branch.

Yes, the answer came back. It is the tree of life. The fruit of this tree is life eternal, immortal, everlasting life. Climb this tree, embrace it, remain fixed to it, and sleep. When you wake up it will be to eternal life.

Then he raised his arms horizontally and shouted out in a clear voice: *not my will but thy will be done.*

You did well the gardener told him. On the previous occasion you said the contrary: not thy will but my will be done!

Sir, he told the gardener, you said I will sleep. How will I wake up?

You will be woken up, the gardener assured him, You will be woken up by the gentle rustling of a woman's clothing. You will be woken up by her presence. You arose out of the womb of a woman. A woman will witness you rising out of the womb that is the tomb, the surrogate form of mother earth.

Who is that woman, Jesus asked.

Miriam, replied the gardener. Miriam, the eternal mother, the eternal lover, the eternal companion. Jesus, you went to sleep on that tree after drinking out of a chalice that offered you unpalatable bitterness. The chalice Miriam will offer you on your awakening in her person will be filled hundredfold with ineffable joy.

Now his mind was a whirl. He was hearing the story his mother told him so many times. He remembered she had spoken of an apple tree and a serpent.

Yes indeed, another voice was saying reading his thoughts. The tree was indeed an apple tree, and as for the serpent, that is me. He laughed again.

Why have you come back? he asked the serpent suspiciously.

Do not worry, I have nothing more to offer you, the serpent said.

You gave me something before and that changed the destiny of the world.

True, replied the serpent, That was the fruit of one tree, the one of good and evil. There is yet another tree, the tree of immortality. Do not count on me to give you its fruit. You will have to get it yourself.

Adam, the serpent said. There is one more thing I must tell you. On the first occasion Eve gave you the wake up call to an earthly existence. The next wake up call she will give you is to immortal life. That Eve has now become Miriam. It is not the form or the name that counts Adam, it is the identity. But to me you will always remain Adam, and she, Eve.

CHAPTER 42 - NATURE OF WOMAN

Jesus was still reminiscing about the creation story. Details were now surging up from his memory and taking form within him. He had emerged from the womb of mother earth held by God in his hand, and then had fallen into a death like deep sleep, until he was awakened by the magnetism of his other self, the flesh of his flesh and the blood of his blood calling him back to wakefulness. This new life that sprouted from within him was the life of Mother Earth, no more as a mother but as a companion and lover.

The life giving force of the Earth, which he experienced had three attributes, those of lover, mother and companion. Firstly, it brings a being into existence. Then it accompanies him on his life journey as companion, be it sister or friend. Then it draws him to unite with it and become one with it so that out of this oneness of form and spirit also called love, life will sprout anew. This threesome out of the one and only Mother Goddess is the Trinity of all earthy existence.

Now the voice was talking to him. It said: it is no wonder then that Biblical wives were sisters really or imaginatively of their consorts. Such is the case of Abraham and Sarah, and Isaac and Rebecca. As for Abraham, he said of Sarah: Besides, she actually is my sister and she became my wife; and it came about, when God caused me to wander from my father's house, that I said to her: *This is the kindness which you will show to me: everywhere we go, say of me, He is my brother*. In one case the father became the husband of his daughters as in the case of Noah and his daughters. He had been witness to these episodes and so had fearlessly proclaimed that women are *daughters of Abraham*.

He had done so against the culture and the tradition of the day. There were rabbis who prayed every day: "I thank Thee, God, that I was not born a Gentile, a dog, or a woman". They were so strict in their observance of the Law they would not even look at a woman. If they sensed that a woman was going to cross their path, they would close their eyes tightly and walk straight ahead. Women were debased Jews, excluded from the worship and teaching of God, with status scarcely above that of slaves.

He had been a rebel teacher, a revolutionary rabbi. He had broken all the laws and rules that applied to Jews, especially to rabbis, regarding women. He had indulged in long discourses with solitary women, and strangers at that. In Judean society of the day, it was a major transgression for a man to talk to a woman other than his wife or children. He had even touched them and had been touched by them. He had cured them even of most intimate sicknesses such as those affecting their menstrual cycle. His love and sympathy towards them was limitless.

Your behavior is totally at variance with Jewish beliefs, customs and traditions, he heard someone say. From where did you imbibe this different ideology?

From Egypt, he heard himself say.

What is it that Egypt taught you that has transformed you into a stranger in our midst, into a revolutionary and a rebel? the same voice continued to ask.

The reality and the nature of the Mother Goddess, he answered.

What is her nature? The voice persisted.

She is Triune, being mother, spouse and companion. These are her inherent attributes, he said.

Never had the Jewish nation of his time witnessed anything ressembling even by far, the apparition of this teacher in their midst. And women reciprocated his love to the very end. The "daughters of Jerusalem" followed Him and wept for Him as they made their way down the *Via Dolorosa* to the summit of the Golgotha hill. His mother and lover stood under the cross and felt his blood as it splattered on their bodies. They had even tasted it as drops fell on their lips. This blood was more real to them than the symbolic blood he had offered to his disciples at the last supper. It was the blood that was oozing out of his body and not the blood offered to the disciples in cups of wine with the taste of wine.

And now a woman's voice arose out of the tumult his thoughts were causing within him. It said: Master, I drank you blood. The previous day you had offered your blood to your disciples in a very palatable and enjoyable form: as wine. What your disciples felt was the taste of wine. What those men of rough and crude stock felt was its inebriating effect. Its real nature they were unable to savour. So strong was its effect that when you led them to the Garden of Gethsamene where you agonized at the thought of the horrendous death that awaited you, they fell into a drunken sleep. Your blood within them had no other working on them except to induce their state of intoxication.

But I, your handmaid, I drank your real blood. It intoxicated me differently: with love, yes with physical love. It was the love that demands a new creation within me, a creation by the power of your Spirit that would be your real body and your blood. My maternal womb will then be the new Holy Grail filled with your life giving blood. It will usher the new creation and the new covenant. Our relationship will grow into a blood relationship, my Lord. What we will create is a blood line which will ensure your presence in this world for all time. This was your last unfulfilled wish.

The predominant appellation of all these female forces in the life of a man was that of 'woman'. That is primarily what this force was, namely: woman. Had not God said: *it is not good for man to be alone*? A man who is alone is an unfulfilled being. It is woman who gives him the sense of fullness and of fulfillment. It is she who conferes on him his sense of identity, firstly on the different stages and scenes of his life, and then as the pathway and gateway to the divine consciousness, where they will be forever united as ONE.

Jesus never called his mother by any other name but that of 'woman'. To Jesus, Miriam was a force superior to any specific role she had taken on herself. She was 'SHAKTHI'. She was womb and life and tomb and life. Womb and tomb were different configurations of the same life giving power. Both womb and tomb took the body within it. Both womb and tomb offered the bodies within them to the breath of the spirit, and as such made them emerge from within them as living beings. It is over the eternal waters of the womb that the life giving spirit of God hovers with the unspoken words: let there be light…and that light is the life of men.

For Jesus, the word woman signified the female nature of the Godhead, the visible God, the only God the mind can envisage as creator of the world. The known goddess of life is woman, the embodiment of mother, the queen of all creation, of the earth and of the heavens. It was of her that the scriptures wrote: *For we know that the whole creation groans and suffers the pains of childbirth.*

As these thoughts occupied his mind he felt the Spirit hovering above him, and he heard a female voice bursting through the unfathomable spaces of the heavens which said: *This is my beloved one in whom I am well pleased.* In that instant was revealed the Eternal, Infinite Godhead, as Mother, Bride and Companion.

CHAPTER 43 - MIRIAM

He was now standing and facing Miriam. They knew that the moment of parting had come. Neither of them dared speak, thus bathing in the stillness of the timeless.

You and I, we are priest and priestess of the Mother goddess, Miriam finally told him. Do you remember the day you were an invitee in the house of a certain Pharisee? You were reclining at the table in his house. Do you remember how I brought an alabaster vial of perfume, and kneeling behind you at your feet, weeping, I wet your feet with my tears and kept wiping them with the hair of my head and anointing them with the perfume. That was how I, as priestess, anointed the body of the living Pharaoh for his death. I was there when you were put to death, standing at the foot of the cross drinking the sacred blood that was oozing out or your body. I helped to carry you to your makeshift tomb.

The next day, not only as priestess, but also and principally as a spouse, I returned to the tomb with costly perfumes, scented with the resin of myrrh, the leaves of aloe, and spices, to anoint your body for final burial. I claimed the right to get it back from where ever it has been secretly laid. Jesus, I visited your tomb thrice to confirm my status as lover, mother and companion. Who else would be permitted to anoint the body of a dead man which would involve his total denudation but his spouse, mother and companion? I claimed total authority over your body and defied the Roman authorities while the disciples who would eventually oust me from my privileged place in your life, shuddered and huddled in fear.

Now memories were flooding his mind. Then thoughts took over. Life is a transition between womb and tomb, the tomb which is itself a passage to a womb. Both womb and tomb are configurations of the great womb that is mother earth. The earth is clay and dust, clay for the arising, dust for the disappearing, both of which are illusions because life is an ongoing, uninterrupted process of ephemeral, transient and evanescent phenomena.

The most recurring of all his dreams was of himself standing by the side of an open tomb, and confronting a woman who was searching for a body among the dead. In her mind she was in a garden of yore being led around by a gardener. He had told her of one who was flesh of her flesh and bone of her bone, who was lying somewhere waiting for her to appear. She was told that the man, the dream of her mind and heart was asleep.

Sir, she was asking him, *tell me where you have laid him so that I could go and find him.*

So had the scriptures foretold: *I sought him whom my soul loveth: I sought him, and found him not. I will rise and will go about the city: in the streets and the broad ways I will seek him whom my soul loveth: I sought him, and I found him not. The watchmen who keep the city, found me: Have you seen him, whom my soul loveth? I found him whom my soul loveth: I held him: and I will not let him go.* It was then she heard her name being called out.

Miriam, he said, and she recognized him.

I found him whom my soul loveth: I held him: and I will not let him go.

He walked down the corridors of his memory, while his imagination conjured up forms, faces and figures of his life. They were not figures of his past because they were there before him NOW. He was now hearing the rumblings like that of a moving vehicle, the vehicle that was time. He was seated by her side.

Mary, he was telling her, very soon I will be leaving you and will be gone. Will our love end with our respective departures?

No, he heard her say. *I will always love you. We will meet again and again as the eons go by. Whether present or absent I will always be by your side.*

Union and separation he learned were two inevitable facets of life. Nothing was permanent. Such was the condition of impermanence. It meant that nothing ever lasted. So it was on the stage of life as regards the forms and the identities which the unfolding scenes of time required.

Miriam, he said, as one last question sprouted out of his mind. You said: we will meet again and again as the eons go by. But will you recognize me when we do meet? He once again evoked their meeting in the cemetery by the open tomb. He saw her confusedly asking him who she thought was the caretaker and gardener of the site for information regarding his body.

There were other episodes rushing in and calling for his attention. He saw himself on the Road to Emmaus meeting with two disciples. They had not recognized him. It was only during the breaking of the bread that their eyes were opened. Yet their hearts were burning while he was talking to them, and opening their eyes to the scriptures in his regard. Then he encounters his disciples by traversing the closed doors and stepping into the room in which they were. He must convince them by allowing them to touch him. He meets them once again seated on sea sand while from their boats they think they are seeing a vision. So the question he was posing to her seemed valid and lingered on his lips.

Jesus, she finally replied. It is true that I recognized you through your voice and your words reverberating in the depths of my inner consciousness, because it is there that reality and truth abide, and not in the outward form. We are both more than mere physical forms. We are the outpouring of the spirit who is the divine consciousness. It is this spirit that leads us to one another.

We were together in eternity as the eternal word and its wisdom. It was through us as one with the creative power of God that the world was made. And then we became differentiated, you as the spirit that hovered over the waters, the mirror of yourself, and I as the reflection of your image and likeness within it to which you transmitted that light which is your life. There can be no image and likeness within the mirror without the one who looks into that mirror. There cannot be one without the other. Your resurrection is nothing but another rebirth within the mirror, the waters of the divine consciousness that I am. And there we both abide until the end of time, you as son and savior and me as your lover, mother and companion. So will it be forever and ever and nothing will ever do us apart.

I will never lose sight of you because I will always exercise on you my triple role as lover, mother and companion. So it is out of me that you will continue to be born and reborn. My motherhood in your regard is so unfathomable that it surpasses everything the mind can conceive in its regard. That mystery lies hidden in the words that I proferred as the Wisdom of the Godhead with which we are both one: *Can a woman forget her suckling child, that she should not have compassion on the son of her womb? Yes, they may forget, yet I will not forget you.*

CHAPTER 44 - PARTING THAT NEVER WAS

✼✼ ✼✼

The parting of their ways now seemed imminent and recollections were pouring into her mind. The night that Jesus agonized in the Garden of Gethsemane, Miriam, her mind tortured with apprehensions, rolled about on her mat. She had a premonition of what was to come, and her mind braced itself to confront the situations as they occurred. To save her the suffering about to befall her, her mind was offering her a strange relief. She dreamed of a very beautiful garden of which she and a man were the custodians. She tried hard to recall the rest, but it was all in bits and pieces now and the very look of her face was enigmatic as she tried to weave them into something coherent. What it was she had really dreamt she could not say, yet she strained her memory and especially her imagination to arrive at a cohesive vision of what had transpired in her dream. It was like trying to reconstruct a very ancient writing, filling the lacuna as best as possible, and trying to imagine what the original text would have been.

And then of a sudden it happened. She remembered the moment that was rising from the depths of her memory like a whirlpool gushing out of the ocean. It was to her like waking up from a dream. She remembered a sleeping human form. It was the form of a male, of a man. But where did she come from? How did she happen to be there? As if in answer to that question her birth was being reenacted before her own eyes. The sleeping man was armed with what seemed to her to be a breast plate of bone that protected his greatest possession, his heart. Then that breast plate, that bastion, that fortress of the heart of man was taking form before her eyes. It was her form, the form of the woman she now was.

But she was distracted, captivated by the form that was lying at her feet. Nothing else mattered to her, but that form, the form her imagination had conjured up in her mind, the form of the male, her mate, her man, that part of her that she felt as being missing in her physical and psychological makeup. It was the form with which the word of God was revealing himself to her. Nothing else would satisfy her but the human form made in the image and likeness of God himself. Now he was there and he was hers.

She had arisen taking her female form from the breast plate that protected his heart. That would henceforth be her role: to protect him and to ensure that he live, that he find all delights, not in a garden devoid of feelings, sensations and thoughts, but in her, the physical embodiment of the garden of all delights. It was she his paradise. Then for the first time she felt being alone with him. It seemed to her that the word of God and his spirit had merged with the form at her feet. Yes, it seemed to her that God was at her feet, at the feet of the woman.

Then her mind rolled forward over eons that were all as an eternal present in an everlasting unchanging NOW. She saw herself standing over the body of a fallen man who only seemed asleep, because in him the word and the spirit of God were alive. The name struck her like a bolt of lightening. It was Jesus. And what is my name? she thought. And then the words appeared in her mind as hewn in the rock. My name is Miriam. *How can that be?* she instinctively asked herself. *Did not God name me Eve?*

What is in a name, the answer came like a wind drifting over the seas of time. What matters is neither the form, nor the name, but the identity. Your identity is that of the primordial woman, the woman the word brought forth with the breath that is the spirit of God.

With a shudder she came back to herself. She saw the sleeping form raise itself up. He was now standing before her in all his glorious nudity like the uncovered sun that had risen in her heart. *You are beautiful,* she told him. *You are my dream come true. Nothing else now matters to me but you. We will live together forever, over ages, over eons, until the end of time. We, the one and the other, will live as one, united as the two missing parts of one body.* She then flung herself at his feet and grasped them in a passionate embrace. *My lord and my God, never will I let you go,* she said.

Then of a sudden the scene changed and she was standing before another man. It was as if nothing had happened and nothing had changed. *My Lord and my God,* she was telling him as she flung herself down at his feet holding them in a tight grasp, in what she thought would be an eternal embrace.

It was then she heard his voice telling her, *no, Miriam, let me go, I have not yet ascended to my father.*

She sensed a change come over him and suddenly seemed so perplexed. *It is my mind playing tricks with me again. I heard you tell me not to touch you because you had not yet ascended to your father,* she told the figure who stood in front of her. To whom was she talking? Were there two men in her life or only one?

Do not hold on to me. I have not yet ascended to my father. I am not what I seem to be. Do not hold on to me because my physical form is an illusion. You were holding on to me, kissing me and caressing me during my earthly lifetime, as actors on the stage of time and space. But now I am in the process of doing away with my flesh. I am being transformed into pure consciousness, divine consciousness, in other words, pure spirit, in the presence of which all else is pure illusion. For thine is the kingdom, the power and the glory, and all else is the void and the emptiness. Outside of divinity there is nothing in man.

Think well, she pleaded with him. *We are one flesh. We cannot tear ourselves asunder by each following a different path. What one decides and does, the other too must decide and do. Do not forget, indeed never forget, that no garden of delights can never offer you the delights that I offer you. I am your garden of delights. As long as I am with you, you will have your delights without end.*

Jesus, you have a choice. You want to do the will of your father. Do you remember his will in our regard? That man shall leave father, mother, brothers and sisters and cling to his woman, because what God has joined no man should put asunder. The words 'no man' includes you, Jesus, and you more than anyone else. Jesus, that is the will of our father. Your place is with me and with no other. The first place where the will of the father should be done is on earth. In heaven that question does not arise.

And now she saw herself leaning against his breast at the last supper. He had taken the chalice into his hands and drunk of it. then she saw him turning to her with the words: this chalice contains the blood of the new testament. Then, as she watched amazed the chalice in his hands was changing form. She was mesmerized at the metamorphosis of the chalice until it assumed its definitive form. It was the form of a woman. To her utter amazement she realized that it was she, the chalice. Quite out of breath she exclaimed: that is me, Jesus, that is me.

Yes, he replied gently, it is you, this chalice, the holy grail, this tabernacle of the new Testament. It is from your body and your blood that the divine bread of life took human form and appeared in the world. You, lover, mother and companion, are the new testament, the testament of my subconscious mind, the realm of my own dreams. This dream, this vision, is not an illusion, Miriam, he said, it is real. In you, with you, and through you, the testament of the Godhead has been revealed to the world.

CHAPTER 45 - FINAL CHAPTER

✣✣ ✣✣

He was now standing on the threshold of the great divide. By his resurrection he had become pure spirit. Yet a part of him was still embedded in the dream reality of time and space. He had seen how a voice, a touch, a gesture had fabricated, each in its own way, a bodily endowment for his spirit. His body was now like the hidden manna that only he who received would recognize, for what it was. Yet he seemed to waver. But she was steadfast and held firm.

Jesus, she said, looking at him entreatingly. Do not go. Once you cross the stillness of the mirror of time you would also have crossed the eternal waters, the repository of the image and likeness of the Godhead. Once you cross the eternal waters you will merge with the un-manifest Godhead: which is a silent, unfathomable, inaccessible and unknowable being. Then the earth will become formless and void once more. She knew that was what he had prophesied through the mouth of Jeremiah: *I looked on the earth, and behold, it was formless and void; And the heavens, they had no light. I looked on the mountains, and behold, they were quaking, And all the hills moved to and fro.*

She felt a doubt simmering within his mind, yet he made bold to say: *Your sun will never set again and your moon will wane no more. The Lord will be your everlasting light and your days of sorrow will end.*

My Lord and my everlasting light, that is you, my Jesus. Should you leave me, both the sun and the moon will disappear from me, and I will be engulfed in darkness. He was listening to her seemingly stoically but she distinctly felt him wavering in his resolve.

Seizing the occasion Miriam continued. Then all that we have achieved by our togetherness would have been undone and brought to naught. Now we live a dream full of hope, a hope that speaks of triumph and an end to the darkness of ignorance. If you forsake the world you will hear the world cry out to you with your own words on the cross: *why have you forsaken us.* Its dream will become empty. It will be devoid of hope, for it is hope that springs eternal in the human breast. If you go, pretenders will step into your form proclaiming themselves to be other Christs. Now can Christ be divided? Can Christ be multiplied?

Her words made him conjure visions of the future when a monolithical institution constructed with the hands of self proclaimed 'other Christs' will ceremoniously and pompously declare itself the spouse of Jesus, thereby usurping what was her destiny, mission and unique prerogative.

Jesus, you are not a mathematical entity or figure, she was continuing. You are a person. And remember you are only half your person. Jesus, your other half is me. The 'other Christs' will lay hold of the emptiness they will confound with your form and fill it with their own. They will lay hold of the half they think is you. But the chalice, the holy grail, the tabernacle, your eternal womb and tomb that I personify, they will proclaim to be an enemy of light. They will make me a prostitute. They will strip of my primordial role of priestess. They will turn me into the eternal repentant sinner for their own ends and their gain.

They will take pleasure in denuding me, and dragging me along the highways and byways of time, with stones in their hands, to push me over the cliff and put me to death in a make-believe assertion and demonstration of their priestly chastity. If you go you will not be there to expose the real sinners and save me.

Jesus, with me, the chalice of your life giving blood, violated and desecrated, they will proclaim an illusion to be the immaculate virgin. They will shower on that illusion all the tiles of heaven and earth. They will make it appear in every corner of the earth and put the magic words into its mouth: *I am the immaculate conception*. They will pay lip service to her while degrading womankind to the role of chattels at their disposal and at their service.

They will ride on the back of that illusion creating a frenzy of fervor and devotion in its regard, while trampling the real living woman under their feet. While keeping their power structure in force on the substance-less rock 'petra' the woman, it is 'petrus' the man, the male of the species, they will proclaim to be the rock foundation of their kingdom, their power and their glory. It is from the fingers of a man that will dangle the keys of heaven.

Jesus, do not try to cross the great divide. Indeed you cannot. We have witnessed this scene over and over again through the ages, through eons. How many times have I wandered through the labyrinthine ways of the pyramids to call your wandering spirit back to your body. How many times have I roamed through Hades searching for you among the shadows. Once they buried you in the Nile, then they cut up your body and had it strewn over the spaces of the earth. But I searched for you, collected the minutest parts of your body, held vigil over you and brought you back to life, to me. They called me Isis and you Osiris. But it does not matter for what is in a name or in a form? Only the truth is eternal and the truth is ONE. And when you were Joseph the patriarch, I as the woman Serach, raised your sarcophagus out of the Nile, so that it would be transferred over the desert through the Exodus, to the promised land and to a new life.

Jesus, how many times have I seen your body borne on bamboo stretchers to cries of *'only God is truth'*, laid on pyres of wood, set alight, and reduced to ashes. Even then I followed your spirit to the banks of the Vaitarna where you stood waiting for the boat to ferry you across to eternal everlasting silence. But yet I brought you back. I collected the all those particles of the ashes of your body, held vigil over you and restored you to life. Jesus, just as Isis did with Osiris the only god-man, and as the daughters of Noah did with their father the only man on earth of that time, so too did I do with your revived body. I received your divine seed within me in fulfillment of my mission as your eternal spouse, the spouse who is your would be mother. So out of my womb were you reborn. As lover, mother and companion I will cling to you until your work of redemption is done and over, until mankind is inundated with that divine light which is the life of God. Only then will the sacrifice we made as Adam and Eve reach complete fruition.

Jesus, I am not deterred at seeing you as pure spirit on the threshold of the mirror of time, the demarcating boundary of the above and beyond, of the great divide. I have seen this over and over again since the beginning of time. But the abyss that is me, cries out to the abyss that is you through the voice of the cataracts, of the eternal waters. As long as I am here, your pure spirit will always hover over the waters that are the moving spheres of the earth, and the chalice of your life giving blood, and you will descend into it, into ME, into me your eternal tabernacle, as the light that is the life of men.

While He was listening to her passionate plea, he felt the same emotions that his two disciples had experienced while he was speaking to them on the road to Emmaus. He was saying to himself: *Is not my heart burning within me while she talks to me?* Now his memory was unearthing memories of happenings beneath the waters of the Nile, and in the sifting dunes of desert. They were erupting as a dormant volcano does, emitting rays of dazzling light. He recalled the death of his form of long bygone time as Joseph the Patriarch, in appearance the son of Isaac and Rachel. He recalled his status as second only to the Pharaoh, how he was mummified, taken over the Nile as honours due to the vice-Pharoah, and his sarcophagus submerged in the waters. He recalled how the old woman Sarach led Moses to the Nile and miraculously recovered his mummified body from the bottom of the Nile.

He recalled his long journey over the desert, just as the spirit of a Pharaoh wandered through the barren world of a desert pyramid. And then his body reached the promised land. During this timeless wanderings he was hearing the *'voice in Ramah…Rachel weeping for her child, because he was no more'*. But what are forms and identities but mirages in the desert of life, the creations of the spirit. All through the timeless eons, a woman kept vigil over him, her head against the boulder of his resting place, waiting until he woke from his deep sleep and recognized her form. And when he did rise up, his real identity surged within his consciousness with the utterance of her name: *Miriam*. As in a dream he heard her tell him as his disciples going to Emmaus had once told him: *stay with me Lord, for it is nearly evening and the day is almost over.*

Shaken to the core of his being he was speaking the very words she had heard over the ages and over eons. He was saying: *Miriam, you think I am going, but where am I to go? I am here. And so will we be, together until the end of time. Miriam, the chalice, the holy grail and the tabernacle that you are, will never pass away from this earth, because you are THAT, the form of the Godhead as the divine mother, lover and companion. As long as you exist, so will I issue out of your womb into life, thereafter only to seek you again and again as lover and companion.*

On hearing these words she flung herself at his feet and embraced his legs, crying out with joy: *Rabboni, Master. You are not ascending to the Father, you are staying with me.* He was now filled with her presence. He saw her and felt the warmth of her embrace. His heart was filled with joy. His heart was filled with love. That countless moment of time clothed with the words 'three days', had he spent within the immeasurable spaces of the tomb and womb of mother earth. Now, like the sun of light and life bursting out of the confines of the great waters, he was issuing forth clothed in dazzling brilliance. He was stretching his hands towards that surrogate form of his eternal mother, lover and companion the earth, and calling out to her with words of untold tenderness and love:

For behold, the winter is past, The rain is over and gone. The flowers have already appeared in the land; The time has arrived for pruning the vines, And the voice of the turtledove has been heard in our land. The fig tree has ripened its figs, And the vines in blossom have given forth their fragrance. Come, come, you all beautiful one, you immaculately conceived one with no stain of ugliness. How beautiful, how sweet, how delightful you are. Arise, my darling, my beautiful one, and come!

Then the heavens were rent with what seemed to be angelic voices that sang: *life is but a dream, life is but dream: you are the dreamer, you are the dream.*

ABOUT THE AUTHORS

Mario Perera is a foremost Western European languages specialist of his country, Sri Lanka. He speaks six of them and translates from four more. He is proficient in Latin and Greek. His university career spans sixteen years spent in universities of Rome, France (Lille) and Sri Lanka. His fields of study were: philosophy, theology, law, applied foreign languages, interpretation and translation. He has already written more than fifteen books. Several of his books were written in collaboration with Laetitia Buczaczer, graduate in law and psychology, now an executive of a leading firm in Lyon.

Mario's professional life was spent in embassies here in Sri Lanka (French Embassy) and abroad (Embassy of Sri Lanka, Paris), He also worked for UNESCO, Paris as a translator. His services as interpreter and translator were availed of by the French government and the government of Sri Lanka as well as by foreign delegations.

Mario Perera is very widely travelled having been several times to the USA, Canada, the major countries of Europe, and to most countries of South and South-East Asia.

A note to readers and well wishers. Please send in your comments to:

mario_perera@yahoo.com

Books by Mario Perera and Laetitia Buczaczer

Fountains of Life – Royal Botanic Gardens, Peradeniya
First Edition : 1992 (Switzerland)

N'Ayez Crainte (Do Not fear) – Le Bouddha et sa Revelation
First Edition : 1999 (Gunaratne offset Ltd., Colombo)

Archéologie et Religions (French) – Archeology and **religions**
First Edition : 2001 (Gunaratne Printers, Colombo)

L'homme et son monde – Man and his world - A treatise on Buddhism
(with Laetitia Buczaczer). First Edition : 2004 (Kandy offset Ltd., Kandy)

Liqueur Sacrée – the sacred liqueur - All about tea **(with Laetitia Buczaczer)**. First Edition : 2006 (Gowriy Printers, Colombo)

Siripala the Cinnamon Peeler
First Edition: 2008 (Godage and Brothers, Colombo)

The Kingdom the Glory and the Power
First Edition : 2010 (Godage and Brothers, Colombo)

The Bhikkhu Light of Lanka – with Laetitia Buczaczer
First Edition : 2012 (Godage and Brothers, Colombo)

English Essays for Advanced Students
First Edition : 2013 (Godage and Brothers, Colombo)

The Beast - a Liberation Theology for Tamils
First Edition : 2014 (Godage and Brothers, Colombo)

Neelkanth – the story of a dream (wih Laetitia Buczaczer)
First Edition : 2013 (Low Cost Publishers, Delhi, India)

The Wrath of Kali – the dark side of God
First edition : 2016 (Godage and Brothers, Colombo)

To Egypt I sent my son Jesus
First Edition : 2015 (Godage and Brothers, Colombo)

The Man Who Died – The Man Who Came Alive
First edition : 2016 (Godage Brothers, Colombo)

www.ingramcontent.com/pod-product-compliance
Lightning Source LLC
Chambersburg PA
CBHW031441040426
42444CB00007B/921